LEADERSHIP AND WEALTH

LEADERSHIP AND WEALTH

JOHN L. HERRMANN

ASQC QUALITY PRESS

LEADERSHIP AND WEALTH

JOHN L. HERRMANN

Library of Congress Cataloging-in-Publication Data

Herrmann, John L., date
  Leadership and wealth / John L. Herrman
    p.   cm.
  Includes index.
  ISBN 0-87389-051-5
  1. Leadership.   2. Organizational behavior   3. Industrial productivity—
United States.   4. Wealth — United States.   I. Title.   HD57.7.H45   1989
658.4'092 — dc19

ISBN 0-87389-051-5

10987654321

ASQC Quality Press
American Society for Quality Control
310 West Wisconsin Avenue, Milwaukee, Wisconsin 53203

Acquisitions Editor: Jeanine L. Lau
Production Editor: Tammy Griffin
Cover design by Walzak Design. Set in Times by DanTon Typographers.
Printed and bound by Edwards Brothers

Printed in the United States of America

Dedicated to all who yearn for pride and dignity, and especially Lois, for her love forever; our children and their mates, for their dreams for tomorrow; and our grandchildren, for their trust in today. Also with recognition to Joseph, Charles, and Arnold.

TABLE OF CONTENTS

PREFACE

I was plant manager of a production plant of a large chemical company several years ago. During that time, our achievements in the plant convinced me that there is a way for America to regain preeminence in the creation of wealth. Our approach resulted in astonishing increases in productivity and quality for the plant, and fulfillment for all of its people. Improved technology and cost control, of course, contributed to our plant's success, but our efforts focused exclusively on the creation of wealth through self-motivation. Any technological or cost control improvements were the incidental consequence of our focus on, and belief in, people.

The solution to our country's loss of prestige, superiority, and profitability in the world trade market may lie in the answers to the following questions: What is wrong with the way we Americans go about living our daily lives? How do our viewpoints affect the way we manage our people resources on the job?

Part of the answers may be found in examining the business trend that started around the year 1900. Management of family businesses and private corporations was transferred from owners to hired professionals. This encompassed the adoption of a military approach to people management — mainly because it was the only successful management model available. In retrospect, this American management trend may have carried its own seed of destruction. That seed was the philosophy of behavior control through fear.

The military focused on the primordial fear for life as a soldier's motivation to submit to authority in the interest of joint survival, which was personally self-motivating. In the interest of corporate profits, industry substituted the more complex fear of job security for a person's motivation to submit to management authority, which was a less personally self-motivating interest. The fundamentally impersonal nature of industry's purpose (profits), and its method of management, largely account for the development of America's somewhat adversarial approach to human relations. Since profit is necessary for businesses to exist, it is the method of management that corporate America must scrutinize for the attendant results.

For many years America's national prosperity afforded her people the basic needs of food, clothing, and shelter. We became a beacon of inspiration for the rest of the world. During the 1920s through the 1950s, aside from our management of technology and finances (in which we excelled compared to other countries), the source of our prosperity was the productivity of the American people. We were productive beyond what management could assure through fear.

The genius of American people productivity was self-motivation; it flowed from our hope for the future, patriotism, and moral certitude that America was *right*. American self-motivation stemmed from trust in our institutions; we were thereby able to acquire a taste for giving of ourselves, which is akin to entrepreneurship in a corporate context. We found pride in our achievements as productive individuals and as a nation. We also found dignity in being shepherds of our American heritage and in feeling that we contributed to the control of our own destinies. We found personal fulfillment in our jobs while simultaneously submitting to management's method of control through fear.

Such pride and dignity have largely abandoned us; in losing them we have been unable to maintain our preeminence in technology, productivity, and quality — particularly so when others in the world have found ways to become more proficient.

Our nation's approach to management did not provide people with continuity in finding pride and dignity in their work, or in feeling that they were an important part of the life of the institutions for which they labored. Perhaps America's management techniques were not intended to address human values.

Today, disillusionment and greed replace hope and certitude. Management's misconceived philosophy of control through fear continues to haunt us. Adversarial relationships between those who control and those who are controlled characterize our institutions. This unresolved dilemma causes the disillusionment and greed to deepen.

This dilemma need not represent our country's destiny. There is cause for great hope that our nation can regain preeminence in creating wealth. What has happened to us is simply an inevitable consequence of our willingness to be motivated by externally imposed fear. This submission to conformed behavior produced managers who, even with the best of intentions, did not avoid limiting themselves to managing and controlling only those aspects of people's performance that could be externally measured and controlled.

True self-motivation, however, includes those human aspects that cannot be controlled and measured; it entails the accommodation of the whole person.

Submission, for any reason, is utterly alien to the uniqueness of America's basic driving force as a nation. For our nation, the salient aspect of that uniqueness is individualism — the individual self-interest of the whole human being. This alienation from our heritage is the underlying cause for management and labor adversarialism and the attendant need to vent job frustration; it is the underlying cause of our general litigiousness.

In contrast, the salient aspect of Japan's cultural driving force is its perception of family. To the Japanese, fear is also a feature, but it is more subtle. It is not fear of job security; it is, instead, fear of rejection as an individual. A Japanese person's submission to avoid societal rejection is less alienating for him or her than is our personal conformity to avoid job loss. Nevertheless, it is alienating to some degree, as witnessed by the popular practice of people "letting off steam" in after-hours lounges and workout facilities. This suggests that the satisfaction of individual wants and self-interests is a driving, universal need of all people.

In the Soviet Union the salient aspect of national uniqueness is also family; however, the Soviet heritage translates perception of family to mean the nation itself as being the only family of significance to an individual. The consequences of family rejection are more severe than in Japan, and opportunities for acceptable attempts to let off steam are less available.

Sweden's salient aspect is individualism tempered by permeative family control at the national level. Options regarding school choice and career destiny, for example, are basically government-regulated. Here, too, there is a need for people to let off steam and express their individuality by methods that fall in between those of the Japanese and those of the Russians.

In contrast, there is much less macro family control in America (with its heritage of cultural focus on the rights and obligations of individuals). What does exist is more dynamic, but becomes less so as the demotivating greed of special interests increasingly changes the very fabric of our culture. (Examples of this include amoral unions; conceited universities; inhumane political parties; inept corporations; and pallid, almost secular, religious groups, to name a few.) To some extent, this reflects the focus of these special interest groups. They focus more on the rights of their constituents than on their obligations. To a greater extent, this reflects the greed of the managers of these groups.

Each nation's heritage is unique, with salient aspects of motivation ranging from unbridled individualism to almost omnipotent family control. Therefore, America must not be unduly influenced by *how* other nations go about doing things; how they do things may be somewhat alien to our heritage — to our source of individualistic strength.

However, *what* other nations do should continue to be of immediate and great interest to us. This is particularly true with Japan's industrial acceptance of statistical quality control — a concept that embraces an essentially natural and moral premise of productivity, quality, and survival through reduction of waste and variability simply for the sake of reducing it. Their concepts of Wa (strength through the harmony of love of man and his products), and Ai (love of a superior for his people) should also interest us.

In studying them, we must be able to differentiate between the concepts and the practice of the concepts. For instance, these concepts are practiced in a stylized, family-centered climate in Japan, but they (or any other concepts) must be practiced in another way in this country — and that other way is what this book is all about.

America's hope for regaining preeminence in producing wealth and profit lies in understanding the fundamental cultural differences among countries and how these differences influence the behavior of their people, and in better understanding our own heritage. This hope may be realized by focusing on, and satisfying, the needs and personal interests of our people, by using this as a motivational force for them to utilize all of their innate, independent strengths. It is the unleashing of these strengths that is American heritage's unique force. Because we have not focused on this force, personal greed has increasingly characterized behavior in the workplace (and elsewhere) at the expense of personal pride, dignity, and self-fulfillment. Our loss of focus is somewhat understandable in light of how big all of our various institutions have become.

Such corporate bigness seems to shift our focus in such a way that our work behavior is a response to our weaknesses as we serve the needs of our institutions. Instead, our work behavior should be a response to our strengths as our institutions serve our needs as individuals and as a people. We seem to be trapped into putting the cart before the horse. This trap can be escaped; unchecked greed need not be a hallmark of corporate bigness.

The self-interest of whole individuals excludes greed and can be satisfied anytime we are allowed by corporate management, political leaders, etc., to help one another unleash the indomitable human spirit that is in each of us. Only then can we bring to a job situation all that there is within us to give voluntarily.

Our human spirit powered the conquest of our continent, the development of our constitution, the evolution of free enterprise, the provision of an education for all, and the exploration of space. There is no logical reason to assume (as some of us do) that the human spirit will not achieve future progress.

It is a question of a reasoned balance working at resolving three particular dichotomies: 1) contentment versus achievement, 2) solitariness versus cooperation, and 3) shortcuts versus fundamental principles. Because corporate bigness has been allowed to squelch the human spirit, Americans focus evermore on the contentment of material things — on working only for their own selfish interest and on taking the easy way out.

We need to reverse this long-range trend of self-defeating focus. We must focus on meaningful achievement, on cooperation, and on principles; we must focus on the human spirit and produce fulfillment (growth) for individuals, thereby increasing quality and productivity through people.

America *can* reverse this trend. It was reversed with astounding results when I worked as a plant manager for a multinational chemical corporation. It was accomplished without spending a lot of technology money, without hiring experts, and without waiting for someone either to tell us what to do or to exempt us from our accountability. Our plant created an evolving balance between behavior control and what we called *conflict control*. Behavior control encompasses management's imposing rules, regulations, standards, procedures, formal performance reviews, and behavior-oriented slogans for enforcing conformity as *the* way for a person to do a job. *Conflict control*, however, is the process of people helping each other to behave as accountable, conscientious adults (to help each other cope with the conflict of change and growth — to strive together for excellence). We came to understand that *conflict control* is the natural and inescapable process whereby the creation of wealth (including profit) through people is optimized. It characterizes a way of life that we eventually called *striving for harmonious excellence*.

There is, of course, legitimate need for some form of behavior control in the work environment as well as in the broader social environment if the significant lessons of history are to be remembered. However, management has bastardized this legitimacy by specifying work behavior with ever-increasing detailed rules and systems.

It was probably done with two purposes in mind. The first purpose was to prevent all surprises in behavior in the interest of a financial short-term bottom line; this has evolved to where evidence of behavior nonvariance, in and of itself, is seen as a significant measure of success. In addition to reflecting management's desire for behavior predictability, this situation also reflects industry's growing passion for measuring and controlling only quantifiable entities. We task analyze, time study, and predict every aspect of a job.

The second purpose appears to have been the avoidance of any evidence of conflict. Management doesn't want people to react disruptively within the system or with each other (neither predictably nor otherwise), so corporations set up and enforce work rules that allow no room for individual or group conflict. Here, too, the motivation seems to be some quantifiable, short-term bottom line.

Unfortunately for American preeminence and business competitiveness, conflict and unpredictability are integral to the human spirit. The process of conflict control focuses on channelling this conflict toward quality, productivity, and people's fulfillment. This is the natural and inescapable way whereby the creation of wealth through people is optimized.

We at the plant "discovered" this process, although we did not articulate it as such, as we went about trying to figure out how to self-motivate ourselves and others. We focused on how we went about managing our behavior. We called this management *leadership*. As we progressed, we learned how to accommodate the whole person. We discovered that success lies in understanding: 1) what productively motivates an individual, 2) how individuals productively relate to each other, and 3) how to utilize small group dynamics to satisfy individual and group needs.

We discovered that self-motivation flows from first focusing on separate individuals and then on small groups. The concept of family in the workplace, when taken to mean something larger than a small group or a few small groups, was not essential to our self-motivation as long as some family did not deliberately prevent it.

The crux of our achievements is not just another management philosophy or motivation theory with accompanying how-to verities. It is much more basic and potent, requiring only a simple and natural form of leadership.

The plant case study explains what we did, how we did it, and under which circumstances. Specific examples are cited, but they cannot be taken as general guidelines to be applied to different circumstances. However, they can and should be taken as illustrations of the viewpoint of jobs, people, and leadership that is America's prerequisite for preeminence.

These examples are oriented toward production. However, the approach we used and our guiding viewpoint are applicable to any function of business or industry, or any other institution or home life — to wherever people work together to achieve a productive objective.

Our viewpoint is not another panacea for all management problems; it is simply a point of reference for understanding and coping with what makes people tick. You may encounter one or two unfamiliar terms relating to leadership and the determinants of human behavior. However, the human behavior *factors* themselves are not new — we are all quite aware of them; it is the *viewpoint* that is important, for it is the required viewpoint for enriching human relationships as people go about the business of living and working together.

It is this viewpoint, I am certain, that will help spell the difference between success and failure as we Americans pursue the destinies of ourselves as individuals, our institutions, and our nation. It has to do with putting first things first. It is a strategic reference point that will unlock the potential of any compatible productivity tactical approach that we may choose to embrace. It is a starting point from which Americans can get back in touch with their tremendous potential.

DEFINITIONS

These definitions are for the concepts found in this book; some are stressed and amplified. The intent is simply to specify meanings that will minimize ambiguity in the communications of those concepts.

1. **CREATION OF WEALTH.** A consequence of any endeavor that adds value to something that exists or conceives something that is original (i.e., an idea or a design) to enrich human beings.

2. **ENRICHMENT.** A facilitator of human growth. It comes in various forms: knowledge, art, love, ideas, tools, etc. It can satisfy certain needs.

3. **ENDEAVOR.** Any human activity aimed at providing enrichment.

4. **WEALTH.** The fulfillment achieved, and the productivity and quality produced, by those involved in the endeavor.

5. **INDIVIDUALS, PERSONS, PEOPLE.** The doers and/or helpers involved in the creation of wealth. A particular person can be either or both at any particular moment in time. DOERS are those who create the enrichment by driving a truck, learning a lesson, restructuring an organization, painting a picture, coordinating an effort, etc. HELPERS are those who influence the behavior of doers, such as relatives, teachers, peers, subordinates, superiors, financiers, owners, etc.

6. **PRODUCTIVITY.** A helper's perception regarding the effectiveness with which the doer utilizes resources — both external resources (i.e., equipment, materials, money, human beings, etc.) and internal resources (i.e., experience, knowledge, desire, health, etc.).

7. **QUALITY.** A user's perception of enrichment; the degree to which it satisfies his or her perception of need.

8. **FULFILLMENT.** A doer or helper's perception of the growth incurred by his or her doing or helping; the specific manifestations of growth are the amount of pride and the amount of dignity achieved. These are also the justification for seeking growth.

9. **BEHAVIOR.** How a person achieves an objective.

10. **BEHAVIOR CONTROL.** Externally imposed behavior proscribing what is *right*; i.e., rules, standards, procedures, formal performance reviews, behavior-oriented slogans, etc.

11. **BEHAVIOR MECHANISM.** The basic human mechanism involved in the creation of wealth; the exact enrichment produced is affected by heredity, knowledge, experience, circumstances, etc. (See CHAPTER ONE, UNDERLYING RATIONALE OF HOW WEALTH IS CREATED for amplification.)

12. **WHOLE PERSON.** Body, mind, spirit, and free will.
13. **BODY AND MIND.** There is physical interaction between them, with the mind directly influenced by the *spirit* and one's *free will*.
14. **SPIRIT.** A universal force for satisfying nature's plan. It reflects what is *right* and evolves according to nature's evolving plan. *Right* is akin to moral and truth. The perception of *right* is filtered in the mind by heredity, education, and experience. What is not *right* is not necessarily wrong, for what is not *right* today may become *right* tomorrow as nature's plan evolves.
15. **NATURE.** The universe in totality; the source of all wealth and all enrichment.
16. **FREE WILL.** The very essence of human life; being uniquely exactly the same thing in each human being, it renders all human beings inherently equal. Totally under the control of the individual, it causes the mind to accept or reject the demands of the spirit. REASON is a product of acceptance. Fulfillment is the objective of the HUMAN SPIRIT (which comprises the spirit and the free will).
17. **GIVING OF ONE'S WHOLE SELF.** What is voluntarily given when the free will causes the mind to accept the demands of the spirit, rendering noncompliance into compliance.
18. **DESTINY.** The consequence of complying to nature's evolving plan and changing needs.
19. **INTERNAL CONFLICT.** Insecurity generated by the spirit when noncompliance exists; it resides in the mind and produces discord in the mind, causing the mind to reject the demands of the spirit unless the conflict is resolved.
20. **INSECURITY.** The subliminal state of internal conflict that influences human behavior, ever present, but changing in intensity depending on the amount of internal conflict that is resolved.
21. **COPING WITH CONFLICT.** Mitigation of internal conflict through the free will.
22. **NEED.** A focus, generated by the mind, to cope with conflict; discord causes the mind to focus on noncompliance and when it does it produces an *incorrect* need; if it focuses on compliance the need is *correct*.
23. **GREED.** An incorrectly perceived need; a lust for money or power and the justification they represent.
24. **CLASSIFICATION.** A simplification, and conscious acceptance of an involuntary judgment, of a person (i.e., greedy, old, smart, sloppy, dumb, careful, careless, loner, clever, eager); an incorrect perception that reflects an incorrect need for justification or recognition, causing interpersonal conflict.
25. **VALUE.** Any immutable standard held by an individual, including a behavior standard.
26. **STYLE.** The predominant manner in which one person interacts with another.

27. **INTERPERSONAL CONFLICT.** A form of external or internal conflict resulting from incorrectly perceived needs (including societal values or needs that are perceived as being not *right*). When it is visible (when it is not yet submerged, producing internal conflict) it can provide visible clues for coping with conflict to achieve pride and dignity.

28. **PRIDE.** A positive feeling about *what* one achieves; it is founded in hope, released by trust, and confirmed by joy.

29. **DIGNITY.** A positive feeling about *how* one achieves; it is founded in the integrity of reverence for nature, released by trust, and confirmed in peace.

30. **TRUST.** The only thing that can mitigate internal conflict; the key to coping with conflict to achieve pride and dignity. It resides in the mind and causes unity in the mind. Only the free will generates trust, causing the mind to accept the demands of the spirit by generating a residual of unity in the battle of unity versus discord.

    The essence of trust is: 1) a conviction that one's mind must accept the demands of the spirit, 2) a conviction that in so doing, one is growing and will find pride and dignity, and 3) a conviction that others cannot prevent, and when possible will help, one's trying to behave accordingly.

31. **STRIVING FOR HARMONIOUS EXCELLENCE.** Seeking a way of life, according to nature's plan, to optimize the creation of wealth through pride and dignity. STRIVING means working very hard at seeking change and at accepting the attendant risks. It precedes pride and dignity. HARMONIOUS means creating wealth through selecting an objective, and accomplishing it in a way that copes with conflict. It proscribes pride and dignity. EXCELLENCE means that the enrichment produced and/or pursued will truly enrich in that it complies with nature's plan. It reflects pride and dignity. "Overenrichment" is no more truly enriching than is the satisfaction of any other need that does not comply with nature's plan.

32. **LEADERSHIP.** A simple and natural approach to facilitate *striving for harmonious excellence* through trust, assuring optimum productivity and quality through pride and dignity. A leader must build trust by holding three viewpoints: 1) people — the viewpoint is that people are equal and different, 2) jobs — the viewpoint is that individuals' jobs exist for the sake of the group, and that the group exists for the sake of individuals' jobs, and 3) leaders — the viewpoint is that leaders must assure change through trust so that people can cope with conflict (and thereby create wealth) and produce more enrichment.

    Firmly holding these three viewpoints transforms a prior "will to manage" into the ability to lead, but a prior "will to manage" is not a prerequisite. However, insight regarding the behavior mechanism *is* a prerequisite.

33. **CONFLICT CONTROL.** The process of people helping each other, through the behavior mechanism, to cope with conflict and thereby to behave as accountable, conscientious adults in the interest of optimizing the creation of wealth. It is integral to the effectiveness of *striving for harmonious excellence*. Its crux is the process of people helping people to cope with conflict. Specifically, that process is: people help people to trust, to seek change, to achieve a *right* objective, to achieve it in a *right* way, to thereby create additional wealth; then, to trust more readily, etc.

34. **TEAM.** A group of two or more people *synergistically striving for harmonious excellence through conflict control*. It must have leadership, but not necessarily a designated leader.

CHAPTER 1

UNDERLYING RATIONALE OF HOW WEALTH IS CREATED

Leadership begins with the recognition that people's primary behavioral motivation is the satisfaction of their physical, emotional, intellectual, and social needs. Such leadership contrasts with management, which merely involves controlling quantifiable measures of performance, and translates to the unrealistic attempt to control people's behavior.

THE BEHAVIOR MECHANISM

As the mind perceives a need, the behavior mechanism is triggered and produces a decision as to whether any action is to occur for achieving an objective. This action may or may not be rational or entail physical activity.

If a person's free will has generated insufficient trust, internal conflict and distress will cause his or her mind to reject the demands of the spirit — rejecting what is *right* to him or her. Even if the need is correctly perceived, either the need will be ignored or the objective and/or method chosen to satisfy this need will not be *right* to him or her. For example, you come home from work and see that the grass needs cutting. On the way home you fantasized about just relaxing and thereby escaping the stresses of the day — nothing wrong with that until you see your lawn. In this instance, assume you decide to ignore the grass. However, you find that you can't relax, knowing the grass needs cutting. Finally you decide to cut the grass, but you tell yourself the edging can wait until next time. You find that just cutting the grass was not very rewarding, but you have resolved to do the minimum because you *are* going to enjoy the relaxation you have earned. However, the peace you were seeking eludes you.

If a dubious objective is achieved, a person will have no personal pride or dignity in his or her accomplishment. A person will experience internal conflict and intensified insecurity because he or she has rejected what he or she believes is *right*. Without question, a person will lack trust in himself or herself and in others when dealing with future conflicts. Failure will tend to breed failure.

On the other hand, if a person's free will generates sufficient trust to cope with conflict — if unity replaces discord — his or her mind will accept the demands of the spirit to render the conflict of noncompliance into the growth of compliance. Incorrectly perceived needs will be ignored and insecurity will be diminished. Correctly perceived needs will be acted on, the objective and

5

the method chosen will be *right*, and the person's free will will allow him or her to give of his or her whole self (mind, body, and spirit). This will reduce insecurity, and a person will find the degree of pride and dignity that is intrinsic to the activity at hand; and he or she will require less help to secure the trust needed to cope with future conflict. Briefly, his or her reasoning will have produced satisfaction in his or her task performance and accomplishment, and he or she will have behaved rationally. For example, in this case you would have recognized, accepted, and satisfied the need to do a thorough job (including the edging). The attendant pride and dignity would have provided the sought-after antidote to the day's stresses.

In giving of oneself, a person gives hope, desire, thought, creativity, concern, curiosity, conviction, determination, and enthusiasm (not to be confused with exuberance). These feelings and traits are integral to self-motivation; they constitute what is sometimes called a good attitude. They are the human basics of entrepreneurship. Therefore, it is quite probable that in addition to attending pride and dignity, these concepts also optimize productivity and quality for the endeavor as well as personal fulfillment for the individual. *Harmonious excellence* is thereby achieved.

Perceptions of *right* will vary among different individuals and countries. Responses will be affected by heredity, individual cultures, religions, knowledge (through training and education), experiences, and circumstances. The monetary value a particular society places on these responses will also vary and reflect its mores, tax policies, financial programs, market influences, and general economic situation.

Although *different* in specifics, *all* acts of people giving of their whole selves are intrinsically *equal* because they are in compliance with nature's plan for satisfying human needs and producing enrichment. Similarly, the *motivation* for giving (the satisfaction of correct needs) is also equal but different (differences in needs).

THE PROBLEM

Two needs are so profound and urgently sought by all people that they can be called longings. The first is a longing for contentment. It is a longing for satisfaction with the status quo and for freedom from needs, insecurity, discord, and change. In effect, it is a longing for freedom from internal conflict (a consequence of noncompliance). It produces fear of, and resistance to, the change that is essential to compliance; therefore, it is an incorrect need. One of its results can be mindless conformity.

In the first instance of the grass-cutting example, having done a minimal job and still seeking contentment with yourself as you are, you are not apt to be in a mood to seek the challenge and intrinsic change of doing a better job at work the next day. You will conform to the minimum expected even though this will be self-defeating. Or you may seek to impose your values on others (if you are in a position to do so) in an effort to find external justification. But you will not really find the contentment you seek through the exercise of power. You are in a downward spiral of increasing insecurity which will continue unabated until you find the trust required to break free.

If insufficient trust exists, the longing for contentment will cause a person's mind (through free will) to reject the demands of the spirit and will intensify his or her insecurity. This is the situation that greed for power or money preys on. This profound need is self-defeating when unmitigated by trust, ultimately causing apathy or stupor, for example.

When sufficient trust does exist, the longing for contentment is not self-defeating, but it *is* self-denying. The mind (through the free will) will ignore it because longing for contentment is an incorrectly perceived need. (As in the second instance of the example, where you decided to ignore relaxing at that time, but instead to do a first-class job on the yard.)

THE COUNTERBALANCE

The second longing is an opposing need of similar strength — the longing for fulfillment — for pride and dignity and, in effect, for compliance with the demands of the spirit; it is thereby a correct need. Its satisfaction is the objective of the human spirit; its satisfaction involves change. Circumstances, culture, environment, etc., will dictate *specific* changes in areas such as family relationships, recreational outlets, job content, job knowledge, personal goals, organizational structure, and priorities. All changes are initially perceived as a threat to contentment, for they initially seem to be abnormal rationalizations of the circumstances at hand.

In striving for fulfillment, a person will fail if he or she lacks sufficient trust and his or her insecurity will be intensified (as when you cut the grass, but didn't trim it). When sufficient trust exists, his or her longing for fulfillment will be satisfied. Trust allows the fear of change to be tolerable through the anticipation and achievement of fulfillment. The elusiveness of contentment and the challenge of fulfillment will prompt a person to continue striving for fulfillment.

People who are the least insecure will make more frequent attempts to achieve fulfillment and will be the most successful; they will generally require less help in reaching the required level of trust. However, since insecurity and the longing for contentment are present in every individual to some degree, everyone needs some amount of help. Those who are the most impoverished mentally, physically, or emotionally will tend to need the most help since they will tend to feel abused.

Help in achieving trust improves the likelihood of obtaining *harmonious excellence* and increases the frequency of trying. As previously mentioned, success tends to breed success. In the first instance of grass cutting, assume your next-door neighbor had observed you cutting the grass and deduced from the way you went about it that you might not edge it. Noticing your ire, and being concerned about that and with the appearance of the neighborhood, he shows up with his edger, tells you he's just had it put into first-class shape and asks if you would like to try it out for him to make sure it is really OK.

THE STARTING POINT OF THE PROCESS

The process of *conflict control* — people helping one another to be conscientious and accountable — begins by understanding how people are alike and equal: motivation, longings, spirit, free will, insecurity, needing help, and giving of the whole self. How people are different must also be understood: heredity in general, culture, knowledge, experience, and circumstantial needs.

It must also be understood that needs can be divided into two categories. The first is the need to be — such as the need for personal achievement; the second is the need to belong — such as the need for recognition. The significance of the need to belong is that it causes a person to seek contact with others; this simplifies the giving and receiving of help. The strength and balance between these two categories of needs varies between individuals and generations, and within an individual in time.

THE BASIC UNIT FOR SYNERGISM

As few as two people can be involved in the process of *conflict control*; two people constitute the basic unit for this cooperative process. At least one person (a doer) must be doing something that will produce enrichment (restructuring an organization, driving a truck, teaching a student, painting a picture, etc.), and at least one other person (a helper) must be helping him or her reach this goal. The trust generated between them results in synergism — a cooperative effort — that otherwise would not have been achieved. The product of such synergism is improved productivity, quality, and fulfillment. This is what happened in the grass-cutting case unless, instead of proceeding to use your neighbor's edger on your lawn, you unpleasantly told him what to do with it.

The helper's purpose is to assure that the doer converts noncompliance into compliance. If the doer is not complying correctly, the helper must increase the doer's trust until: 1) the doer decides to do something *right* in the *right* way, or 2) the doer accepts an objective provided by the helper as being *right* and then figures out a way that is *right*, or 3) the doer comes up with his or her own objective and accepts, as *right*, a method provided by the helper.

Whatever assistance the helper provides must be as general as possible, and he or she must accept the doer's perception of *right* with respect to specifics and details. The helper is in the position of having to mix idealism — inspiring trust, goal setting, and method selection — with pragmatism — realizing that spelling it out is self-defeating.

The doer's decisions regarding what and how is *right* may not result in complete success. It is not the helper's purpose to assure complete success. If the optimum job productivity, quality, and fulfillment is to be achieved in the circumstances at hand, the helper must give just the minimum amount of assistance required to trigger the doer's conversion from noncompliance to compliance. (Doers learn to do their jobs better, and find pride and dignity in their accomplishments when they do what they can on their own.) The helper's objective is to help the doer unlock his or her creativity, but not to direct its course (although some direction may be required). To do otherwise would restrict the doer's perception of *right* and impede his or her enthusiasm and giving of himself or herself, and would thereby make optimum success impossible. The helper would have to assure another opportunity for the doer's next effort; had the helper not hindered the doer, he or she might not have to make a second effort.

Similarly, the doer must allow the helper to render his or her help in ways that seem *right* to the helper. The form of help given will depend upon the helper's interpretation of the job circumstances. The helper may prod, suggest, encourage, discipline, remove restrictions, teach, or whatever. The helper (and also the doer) will be dealing, in effect, with various dichotomies (contentment versus fulfillment, beliefs or values versus pragmatism, feelings of revelation versus reason, accountability versus freedom, etc.). The helper may give the doer individual attention or ask others for assistance. In a sense, the doer and helper are each other's customer — the doer's need for help is an "order" that the helper supplies, and the helper's desire to help is an "order" that the doer supplies.

The simplest and surest way to help begins by the doer asking for assistance. In any event, the doer's behavior should be observed for specific aspects that appear to reject the demands of the spirit — behavior, for example, that appears to be limiting productivity. The helper reasons the sort of help that may be needed; it is not a time-consuming process — it only takes a moment.

The helper, however, must be careful not to let any prior job evaluations or judgments (specifically any prior classifications) of the doer bias his or her deliberation. The helper must also be careful not to allow his or her personal work style, values, or prejudices affect this deliberation. In effect, the helper must strive to put himself or herself in the doer's place. All that is required to do this is honest concern and common decency.

In order to help, the helper must see in himself or herself a need to help. He or she must care enough about the behavior of the other person or the performance of the group. The helper must take the time to help, to accept the risk of interpersonal conflict or personal rejection, and to commit to coping with any conflict that may arise. The helper's own need to belong is the catalyst for such caring. If the helper does not strive to help the doer find sufficient trust, the help he or she attempts to give and how it is given will not be *right*. In effect, the helper will need help in order to help.

The degree to which the helper's insecurity has been diminished previously will proscribe the effectiveness of his or her caring. It will determine the helper's ability to lead by influencing his or her ability to help. The intensity of his or her insecurity will depend largely on the extent to which *conflict control* has permeated his or her work environment.

It is unlikely, however, that any environment involving people is ever in itself either absolutely enabling or absolutely disabling. It is unlikely that any environment can be absolutely one kind — such as *conflict control* — or another — such as behavior control. It is a question of degree.

Nonetheless, through the need to belong, the basic unit or group for synergism — a doer and a helper — helps both of them to achieve a common stake. (The unit exists for each of them.) The common stake is the pride and dignity that accompanies efforts to satisfy correctly perceived needs by the doer and the helper *striving for harmonious excellence through conflict control*. Through this striving process, the amount of help required for future coping will have been reduced, and future striving will have been facilitated.

The process of giving and receiving help may be a difficult and chaotic undertaking. The outcome can be neither predicted nor controlled. Even so, it is a fundamentally natural, simple, essential, and effective process that becomes stronger as the basic unit of two people is extended.

EXTENSION OF THE BASIC UNIT

If three people comprise the group, any particular individual's needs in a *conflict control* climate are apt to be more quickly identified since two people may be giving help. Similarly, any one individual is more likely to be able to give help. As the group size increases, its synergism increases even more.

If the group members have jobs that are nearby or interdependent, additional synergism can occur. Proximity eases observation; interdependence allows job content and employee performance to provide clues for making changes more cogently, reducing conflict, and achieving fulfillment through effective deduction of tactics and strategies.

Synergism is also affected by other factors such as physical realities of the job function and location, by insecurity levels of individual group members, and by the climate of the work environment. A person's desire and ability to help others will be affected by the amount of behavior control imposed on him or her (roughly, the degree to which *conflict control* does not characterize a person's work environment) and by his or her own insecurity (the amount of help a person may need). These limitations restrain the maximum size of the group and the amount of synergism possible.

Enlarging the group beyond its optimum size will diminish synergism through failure to cope with people's conflict. Optimum group size depends on specific situations and conditions and is found through experience. Optimum group size for a particular department or office may change constantly because of personality and expertise variables, as well as other variables.

THE BASIC GROUP FOR SYNERGISM — A TEAM

A group behaving synergistically is a team. Teams provide further synergism when they develop team goals. These goals need not be developed formally or articulated per se. *Conflict control* produces informal understandings (goals) that generate far more significant results than what is achievable with only formal goals. Formal goals tend to become too structured and detailed: They tend to proscribe *right*, thereby demotivating people.

When individuals focus on a team goal and release enough of themselves through trust, they grow through having their needs met with dignity and pride. They experience self-worth through success. They tell themselves that the team goal was worth achieving and that they achieved it well. In effect, they experience growth (and thereby move toward their destinies) through group participation (through their existing, in effect, for the group). To grow through team goals, people must perceive the general objectives and methods to be used as *right*. The *specifics* must be the result of the give-and-take process of the helper-doer relationship.

In encouraging the satisfaction of needs through team goals, a *conflict control* climate heightens an individual's awareness of the goals of the endeavor and his or her contribution toward their satisfaction. Consequently, meaningful team goals abound in a *conflict control* climate, being less proscriptive and more informal and dynamic as they satisfy each team member's perception of *right*.

An individual's needs — including incorrectly perceived needs such as imposing one's values on another person, and correctly perceived needs such as learning to write more effectively — that are not satisfied through teams and team goals will still demand satisfaction. Growth through teams, however, tends to render them subliminal for longer periods of time, to modify them, or both. Nevertheless, the satisfaction of *any* correctly perceived need (whether it be individual or group, in essence) will further enhance synergism on the job.

Thus, team goals can be oriented toward the strengths, weaknesses, or needs of an individual, a job, the team members, the team assignments, or the overall endeavor. When they are acceptable, challenging, and inspiring from both an individual and team perspective, team goals become pervasive and they can be called the culture as long as they continue to be *right*. They are then an enduring, visible feature of the climate of the endeavor and are an enduring source of synergism.

The culture in the case study presented in this book was "professionalism." Professionalism permeated all that we accomplished, including human relationships. It was the plant's consummate societal base upon which a true balance of individual and team needs and perceptions of *right* could be built. Professionalism constantly facilitated the practice of *conflict control*.

Such goals, though powerful, are rare. Goals that are intended to be the culture often do not contain all of the required attributes. They then end up merely as standards against which behavior is evaluated, because they are perceived by the people they affect as simply another form of behavior control.

Behavior controls usually go beyond their only true justification — to help people learn the meaningful lessons of history. Instead, behavior is prescribed and detailed so that all mistakes will be avoided (in order to increase *control* of productivity) rather than simply influenced through the knowledge that improves comprehension (to *improve* productivity) to avoid catastrophic mistakes.

Typical behavior controls are self-enlarging and demotivating. They unnecessarily proscribe *right* and stifle the person's free will, causing consequences leading to management responses that are even more rigid and detailed controls of behavior. They are a product of the fear of those who impose them — a product of fear of conflict and disruption. They are nothing more than a desire for behavior predictability — a longing for contentment. They are the springboard of greed and the grist of demotivation.

At times, however, goals must be imposed — sometimes when circumstances are totally unexpected or traumatic, and sometimes simply because of the nature of particular individual, team, task, or corporate needs. If behavioral control is *not* also imposed, and if there is sufficient trust for the goal to be perceived as *right*, the result will still be optimum productivity, quality, and fulfillment.

THE KEY CONDITION

Trust is powerful, yet fragile. It is the basis for self-motivation, yet insecurity can overwhelm it at the slightest provocation. Therefore, if the creation of wealth is to be optimized, trust must always be maintained at the highest possible level.

The key condition for establishing and maintaining trust is that *conflict control* must always be the societal value of the endeavor. It must never be abandoned for some other value. In the grass-cutting case, if you had perceived that your neighbor could not be trusted to care about your sense of *right* — if he had merely threatened that you had better do a better job of tending your lawn and that when you were finished edging you were going to take your eight-inch shears and trim any remaining blades of grass *or else* — you most certainly would have told him what he could do with his edger and both of you would have deepened your own insecurity.

Other individual and endeavor values do exist, of course, and legitimately demand satisfaction, but they must be kept in perspective because *conflict control* is the only catalyst for all achievement through people. If the individuals or teams do not assure this through leadership, then the managers of their activities must do so. However, to look *outside* their departments for assurance would be unrealistic; other managers would not be familiar with the current needs of the people. As the basic group for synergism, a team can also be the basic group for assuring leadership. It is then called a *conflict control* unit (which can be made up solely of a single team or, if necessary, can be made up of several teams and their operations manager).

Conflict control continuity *can* be assured even in a relatively hostile environment, as demonstrated in the case study. Setbacks may be inevitable, but the case study shows they can be overcome and some degree of momentum *can* be maintained.

SUMMARY

Optimization of the creation of wealth through people is governed by an inexorable behavior mechanism. Two profound human needs directly impact the output of this mechanism. Optimization occurs only through the process of *conflict control*, which synergistically utilizes the mechanism. The overall way of life that the process enhances is called *striving for harmonious excellence*. The process requires only that a simple and natural approach to leadership be allowed to flourish.

REFLECTION

Such leadership should be more natural for Americans (and should therefore allow us to excel beyond all others) because there are a number of parallels between the concepts that comprise *conflict control* and its leadership, and the concepts that make up our American heritage. Both entail a way of life characterized by *striving for harmonious excellence*, as shown by the following parallels:

Conflict Control Concepts	*American Heritage Concepts*
• Striving for harmonious excellence	• America is a way of life
• Trust enabled by free will	• In God we trust
• *Right* goals and methods	• As God gives us to see the right
• Accepting risk of change	• Faith in the future
• People are alike	• All men are created equal
• People are different	• Rugged individualism
• Individual needs	• Individual rights and obligations
• Group needs	• Majority rules
• Behavior control inadequacies	• Best government is the least government
• Helping others	• Income redistribution
• Teams for people to help others	• Crown thy good with brotherhood

Countless other illustrations exist in our history, such as Lincoln's "conceived in liberty and dedicated to the proposition that all men are created equal," and Eisenhower's "we must live with mutual respect and love." It would appear that we have ignored such thoughts only at great potential peril.

Our unique American heritage, fundamentally moral in its focus on the rights and obligations of individuals, indeed points toward *striving for harmonious excellence* as the way of life required for America to achieve its destiny (which is to pioneer the trail that leads each person to growth and thus toward his or her individual destiny). An integral part of America's destiny is for Americans to optimize the creation of wealth through people through *conflict control*.

JOHN L. HERRMANN

CHAPTER 2

CASE STUDY

THE CIRCUMSTANCES

1. Certain activities that began at the outset of the case study, but continued beyond the end of the case study, will be called the experiment.
2. The experiment occurred in a production plant that operated around-the-clock with a total of 60 people and that generated sales of $150 million.
3. The people who were operators and the maintenance craftsmen were hourly paid people who were represented in bargaining by five unions; pay or promotion as recognition of excellence per se was not possible for them.
4. The output performance of the plant was a matter of keeping the plant running and at as high a rate as possible; the process was capital intensive.
5. The plant was involved in a mature business, but one in which there was still active competition and in which there was continuous technological evolution (the lifeblood of survival) which sometimes altered the products manufactured; it was a tough business to be in.
6. The plant was one in a complex of 80 plants, and the complex was part of a major multinational corporation; the financial, physical, and people resources required for success were available.
7. In terms of cost, safety, output, and quality performance, the experiment had to produce results on its own and from the beginning if it was to survive; there was no guaranteed sanction or commitment from higher management.
8. The experiment was conducted long before the surfacing locally of concepts such as participative management, management by objectives, evolutionary training, quality circles, statistical quality control, zero defects, just-in-time production, Japanese cultural superiority, etc., but their utilization — particularly statistical quality control — might have amplified the results.

BACKGROUND

The plant represented a major chemical technology development and had been fully onstream for two and one-half years at the outset of the experiment and the case study. Output rates were good; quality and safety were not as good, but were headed in the right direction.

In years one and two of the plant's operation, large capital expenditures (5 percent of original capital each year) had been made to eliminate quality and safety bottlenecks and to increase production. It was with the coincidental fruition of that effort that the experiment began in year three and continued into year eight. The case study ends in the early part of year six, however, to provide a stable base for comparative quantitative performances. Later in year six, the plant's performance was changed by two events in such a way that performance change could no longer be ascribed to the experiment alone. These two events were a major change in the plant's technology and a major change in general economic conditions.

At the onset of the experiment, there had already been a number of attempts to improve productivity through people rather than through technology alone. One such change made during that period, and that continued all during the ensuing experiment, was the hourly ringing of three bells over the public address system (one each time for safety, quality, and output). No one liked this, and many appeared to resent it, but it did remind everyone of where and why they were there. This was especially effective in terms of the main objective — safety performance.

Because I had imposed the bell ringing on them, it allowed them to focus their frustrations regularly on me, the plant manager, rather than on themselves or others. Imposition of changes by plant management was typical of the period prior to the experiment even though some of the changes had been previously discussed with a few of the people.

In general, nontechnology changes revolved around communications. These changes included team-action workshops, increased supervisor-supervised contacts, motivation literature distribution, plant newsletters mailed home, and formal annual performance reviews. The intent was to keep people informed, and presumably involved in their performance improvement. In doing so, I believed that I was operating on the leading edge of motivation theory.

Slogans were also imposed on the people:

- Do not be a part of the problem but do be a part of the solution.
- Do it now.
- Do it right.
- The problem is always a thing and never a person.
- Upward and downward with compliments and criticisms.
- Protest the rising tide of conformity.

Thirty such changes were made prior to the experiment. Morale and performance improved somewhat after each change, but I noticed that each improvement was short-lived. The only real compensation for all that effort was that morale and performance did not deteriorate, as it did in the other plants within the complex.

This period of imposed change culminated in an event that occurred halfway through year three. It was the event that triggered the experiment.

THE TRIGGER

A three-month strike by all of the unions was the triggering event. During that time, the plant, like all others in the complex, continued to operate by substituting salaried personnel for hourly personnel. Some people felt that the plant's technology at last would be treated with the respect it deserved, thereby improving plant performance.

After one week on the job, however, the salaried people looked, sounded, smelled, and behaved exactly like the people they had replaced. Further, it was only after almost three months on the job that the output and quality of their production finally equalled that of the people they had replaced. It was obvious that, in terms of creating wealth through plant operations, operators and craftsmen were intrinsically equal in worth to salaried people. Their productivity, quality, and fulfillment were proscribed by their jobs and the work climate rather than by their personal attributes.

Given the physical layout of the plant and the provisions of the union contracts, however, not much could be changed in terms of specific job duties. In terms of *general* job content and working relationships, though, there appeared to be considerable opportunity for changes that could improve all plant job performances. For example, there was nothing contractually or physically to prevent people from meaningfully observing and talking to each other while at work.

THE EXPERIMENT IN GENERAL

After the strike was over, in the latter part of year three, I began a one-on-one campaign to build trust. I wanted to deal with our commonly used behavior control approach for improving job performance and its usual results. This approach had produced invisible walls around each job and there were gaps between the walls of one job and another. The people observed the walls as they were supposed to — they tried to follow their job procedures to the letter. Since no behavior control scheme can successfully detail and regulate all situations, these gaps allowed things to go wrong for which no one felt accountable. Typically, these mistakes produced interpersonal conflict and insecurity and usually brought about additional behavior control.

I set out to convince each person that, as a plant manager and as an individual, I believed that each of them was of intrinsically equal worth to the organization and that each of their jobs was crucial to the plant's success. My gambit was that if people were treated as if they and their jobs were perceived as important — and that they became convinced that what they already "knew" was, in fact, so — then the walls might eventually disappear. I ultimately did convince each individual of my sincerity and the walls slowly but surely came tumbling down.

I pledged to each person that changes would be made in interpersonal working relationships, but that if an individual became convinced that any particular change was not *right* in his or her view, then it would be abandoned. A few changes were indeed abandoned. I was again given the benefit of the doubt and was believed and trusted.

That trust was almost never betrayed, and was never betrayed deliberately. On that basis, I eventually became known as a manager who believed what he said, who carefully said what he believed, and who cared enough to keep his word on matters important to his people. Along the way, I learned to not let my personal values and natural style jeopardize this reputation. I similarly learned to avoid classifying people. In being concerned for, and trustworthy to, others' growth (to their finding pride and dignity), I helped them trust that they could and should do what they personally perceived as *right*.

Nevertheless, a proposed change was often met with skepticism. If it seemed to me that it would be eventually accepted, the change was implemented. Those who liked it usually were able to help the others perceive it was *right* for them also; when they were not, I would step in.

Eventually, many of the proposals for change originated with the others — not me. In fact, the vast majority of the changes that dealt directly with operating the plant did originate with others. People began talking more *to* each other and less *at* each other when they realized that these changes unconditionally unlocked their potential for achievement of pride and dignity. Their respect for each other and their trust in each other began to grow. Conspirators and adversaries became teammates who shared in wealth through change.

The plant performance reflected this. People began to feel that it was *their* plant and that its destiny was in *their* hands. Trust was mitigating the unresolved conflict that had been caused by the work environment of behavior control. People helped people, and hope for the future replaced the unresolved conflict of the past. People *behaved* as the responsible people that they had been all along. The human spirit was increasingly helped to exert itself.

This progression toward, and immersion in, *conflict control* manifested itself by:

- A brighter look on people's faces, and a more confident posture.
- A growing feeling by me that I did not have to "boss" — I could be relaxed, creative, and fulfilled by helping others.
- Hearing less "they" and more "we" and "I," and less "want" and more "can do."
- Erratic plant performance became more dependable and predictable.
- A slow, steady shift in perceived justification, from greed to mutual respect and job gratification.
- The setting of records for quantifiable measures of plant performance.

EXAMPLES OF CHANGE

The first change made during the experiment was traumatic. This is not necessarily the best way to start, but I believed this change was necessary under the circumstances. It was a change in the operators' shift schedule, and it unavoidably threatened comfortable social habits. It threatened car pools, hierarchy perks, scheduled days off, vacation schedules, etc.

It was most threatening to the one-on-one trust that had just been established. I gambled that some of the many desirable features of the proposed schedule (such as four consecutive days off once every four weeks), plus an intensive effort to sell the rightness of the idea would be sufficient encouragement for successful *conflict control*. This effort was neither easy nor quick, but it did win the gamble.

The problem with the old schedule — which was the typical one used in the complex and which seemed immutable to the defenders of the union contracts — was not its *efficiency*, but rather that it amplified the lack of worker accountability produced by the invisible job walls. Any two shift jobs on the same shift did not change shifts on the same day. Any resulting interpersonal conflict often was not resolved; it could be submerged for the short amount of time that would lapse before one of the adversaries would change shifts. This tendency to bury conflict between some shift people also carried over to people who relieved each other on the same job, even though the brief opportunity for such conflict occurred only once a day for any particular set of two people.

With the proposed schedule, all the jobs changed shifts on the same day or within one day. This resulted in a group of people working together for approximately five consecutive days, with one to four days off at the same time (depending on the shift), and then working together again. Under these circumstances, interpersonal conflict could not be avoided or ignored as easily; therefore, this shift schedule should make it easier to accept the fact of conflict and then to cope with it. It did exactly that, and tended to carry over to interpersonal conflict between people who relieved each other on the same job.

Significantly, this change was the key to team cooperation becoming a characteristic of plant management, and thereby it was also a key to *conflict control* becoming *the* plant societal value.

I allowed four weeks for the people to debate the merits of the proposed schedule. At the end of that time, positions had polarized — two thirds of the people were for it and one third were against it. Discussions continued to be emotional. After the four-week period the proposed schedule was immediately imposed.

This was the beginning of what quickly became shift teams. Each shift team comprised not only operators, but also the shift supervisor and some of the plant craftsmen. It also comprised a technician and a technical person (people who, nevertheless, still didn't normally work evening and graveyard shifts, or on weekends). Also associated with a team, but not an actual member, was one of the plant's four function managers — production, maintenance, quality, or technical. With the exception of myself, every person in the plant — including the secretary and the janitor — was a member or associate of a shift team.

The team on the day shift was called the operating team and its technical person was called the duty man. The first thing each morning, this team did all the general decision making regarding the next 24 hours' plans for operating rates, maintenance work, shutdowns, technology improvements, quality improvements, safety improvements, supply purchases, etc. The duty man immediately reported the plans either to a group comprised of the plant manager and the four function managers on normal workdays, or to the team's function manager associate on weekends and holidays. The duty man spelled out his team's plans and, in return, was given whatever advice or encouragement needed to help assure success. Team plans were rarely vetoed.

In effect the operating team was responsible for planning the nonroutine activities of the other shift teams. Formerly, this involved recommendations from the shift supervisor to the production manager, and sometimes to me before final decisions were made. Thus, two layers of management were eliminated from normal decision making.

Except for my attendance at the daily managers' morning meeting, the operating team's function manager associate performed all of my plant manager operational and external duties that the work climate would permit. The function managers had the time to do this because the supervisors who formerly reported to them now reported to me. This was not a burden to me since the teams were making most of the decisions, and it helped me to keep in touch with what was going on.

In addition to the four regular shift teams, there was a fifth shift team, the relief team. The small group (the shift supervisor and two operators) which had performed relief duties for other people's normal days off, sick leave, vacations, etc., was expanded until it became a full-size team with six operators and a supervisor, but without the additional nonshift personnel. This expansion increased cost, but the primary purpose was to provide time to the other shift teams for expanding their accountability. Eventually, job restructuring, an incidental result of *conflict control* and attrition, reduced the number of jobs by one and the number of operators by five.

Another unplanned result was that each shift team acquired its own personality and related specialty. Each team was still accountable for the basic plant operation when it was on the job, but each then began to place its own special emphasis on certain aspects of the operation. One team focused on housekeeping, one on quality, one on output, and one on supplies; the relief team focused on safety and cost. Teams, like people, turned out to be different as well as alike. This sometimes produced something commonly called competition. In reality it was simply interteam conflict, but the teams usually were able to resolve it.

Each team's special emphasis also provided both a focus for plant improvements and a new dimension to the plant's challenge to itself, its teams, and each of its people — namely, "professionalism."

The creation of the relief team eventually allowed a reduction in personnel, as previously noted. It allowed the two lowest classified jobs to combine into one higher classified job, eliminating one job per shift. This new job was the same classification as two of the other existing jobs and provided job flexibility in spite of traditional but unspecified differentiation. Also, the total labor cost for operators was reduced to a slightly lower level than existed prior to the expansion of relief people.

The shift teams constituted what can be called horizontal slices of the organization, but vertical slices also existed. Area teams were one such example. Each area team was composed of all operators from all shifts who worked a particular plant area. Added to these teams were those whose expertise focused in that particular area — craftsmen, a technician, and a technical person. Shift supervisors were not part of these teams; instead, they comprised a shift supervisors' team.

The charter of the area teams was to improve productivity and quality in their area and to foster fulfillment and growth for their members. The teams lent an operationally atypical context for focus and significance to otherwise routine contacts among members. The activities of the area teams complemented those of the shift teams.

During one of the area team meetings, an operator indicated that he wanted the assignment of fine-tuning and implementing the recently developed solution to an area problem the team had identified. This assignment typically would have been given to the technical person. The operator's request represented one of the few situations that required my prior approval.

The operator was pulled from his job and temporarily replaced by a relief person whenever necessary while on the project. When the project was finished, the operator had done a great job and was glad that he had made the effort, but still preferred his regular job. The operator, the technical person, the relief person, and others grew from the experience of that project.

The project goal was to eliminate a piping bottleneck that involved a sizable portion of the area. The operator proceeded to lay out and detail the required solution, one which he would have to operate later. The technical person helped him write the formal specifications and complete the paperwork.

The operator then ramrodded the fabrication of the required equipment, the ensuing shutdown of the operation, the installation of the new equipment, and the demolition of the old equipment. The project came onstream on time, under the cost estimate, safely, and without delay in meeting design performance — certainly atypical of most plant projects.

At the end of the project it was obvious that the operator and the technical person were different in terms of training, skills, and experience — but less so than at the beginning, just as they were less different at the end of the strike than at the beginning. It was equally obvious that they were creatively alike in the visualization of the detailed solution and in terms of desire, concern, and dedication. This reinforced my strike period observation that people's performance is limited by an inherent weakness in the system — by management's viewpoint of jobs and people — and not by an inherent weakness in people.

The area teams also proved to be alike as well as different. Some area teams intrinsically had more mechanical problems than others; some had more communication problems than others. Three teams elected to meet after hours at the plant — two teams with overtime meals provided by the cafeteria, while one team opted against meals. Two other teams elected to meet in local restaurants with meals funded by petty cash.

Many changes other than team establishment occurred. The following list briefly shows some of the changes our plant instituted:

1. Operators simplified their written work procedures, eliminating unnecessary behavior control details.
2. Salaried people worked flexible hours (core hours were 10:00 a.m. to 2:00 p.m.).
3. All craftsmen were allowed to weld, not just the boilermakers.
4. Operators and craftsmen administered their own overtime within the intended, rather than the written, constraints of the union contracts.
5. The person to whom a safety incident occurred wrote it up and chaired the subsequent investigation, rather than the supervisor.
6. Operators and craftsmen ordered their own parts and supplies and monitored the inventory.
7. Operators performed the quality tests required in their area rather than sending the sample elsewhere to be analyzed.
8. Operators performed minor maintenance when appropriate.
9. Hard-to-get field information was obtained regarding customer enrichment.
10. Repetitive physical and mental drudgery was minimized whenever possible through a computerized schedule of miscellaneous duties.

In all, 90 changes were identified in the first 10 months of year four alone! A few were originated outside the plant, some were originated by me, some by the seeds I planted, and many by all the other people in the plant.

One summer, a technical person asked to work as a team shift supervisor to determine if he should alter his career path. This freed a shift supervisor to relieve function managers and other shift supervisors during the heavy vacation season. It also allowed the supervisor to become better acquainted with the technical man's job since not all of the technical work could be postponed. Several people became accomplished in new areas and broadened their expertise through valuable on-the-job experience that summer.

In another instance, operators and craftsmen began screening candidates for job openings. A candidate's job classification and seniority were the primary factors in determining who from within the chemical plant complex would qualify to fill the opening. The operators and craftsmen, instead of a supervisor, took the candidate on a plant tour, thereby influencing the candidate's decision by what they said or didn't say to him and how they treated him.

OTHER DEVELOPMENTS

Two other developments occurred, but were not implemented during the case study. They illustrate that a *conflict control* climate leads to a consideration of concepts other than those directly related to interpersonal relationships. These changes nevertheless encouraged people to trust.

A development that began in year four reflected a viewpoint of jobs. It was called Job Scopes. Six Job Scopes covered the entire organization. Each scope was one page long, and the first section of each Job Scope was identical to the others. It briefly described what any person must keep in mind and do on any job to utilize his or her full potential, thereby achieving optimum fulfillment (personal growth and destiny). These included striving for excellence, coping with conflict, understanding the true significance of that job, acting professionally in all that is done, and so on.

Job Scopes then grouped all of the organization's activities into six organizational layers, or spheres. At this point each Job Scope became unique. Each sphere contained five general types of activities — anticipate..., control..., assure..., etc. The last division broke down the general activities into particular activities (which differ from one another in the areas of marketing, production, technology, and research). Generally, it is after this point that typical job descriptions, and their behavior control guidelines, begin.

Even though we used only six spheres to conceptually cover our large corporation's organization, this approach prevented the job duties and accountability of any one sphere from occurring in another sphere, except for interpersonal relationship responsibilities. Layers of people and their reports, whose function was fundamentally to merely summarize what those below them had done, were removed from the operations organization. This included the two previously noted layers in our plant. Among other things, Job Scopes enhanced the sense of accountability in everyone; even though it was not spelled out in detail, responsibility was more visible to individuals; this nurtured their longing for fulfillment. Also, when accountability is clear in a *conflict control* climate, responsibility is accepted, and this tends to discourage unproductive empire building by staff "experts."

The other development reflected a viewpoint on people. It was called EPAM (every person a manager). We began developing it in year five. It seemed logical that if an individual was to manage his or her own destiny through growth, then the individual certainly should be able to determine his or her next pay raise. EPAM was a formula for doing just that.

It involved a multiplier for the individual's Job Scope sphere(s), and a base pay number for the current year and location. It also included input from the supervisor, peers, customers, suppliers, and the individuals themselves. EPAM allowed people to include all of their personal and team needs, goals, and achievements.

Unlike Job Scopes, EPAM was never implemented plant-wide because of our plant's external climate. It was nevertheless quietly applied to a few test cases and appeared to be quite viable; it was interesting food for thought for all of us.

I should point out that all of the changes we have discussed, with the exception of the creation of the shift teams (which I had imposed), occurred naturally as a reflection of the plant's evolving climate of growing trust and productivity. There was no grand master plan then or at any time thereafter.

OTHER OBSERVATIONS

From the beginning, my office was not located at the front of the building; my secretary, the reception room, and the conference room were located there. It was located at the rear of the building, next to the plant entrance. A lot of pedestrian traffic moved to and from the plant at my location, which meant I could observe the faces and postures of various operators, craftsmen, supervisors, technicians, and technical people throughout the day. I "saw" the pulse of the operation through everyone's body language. My office was tied into the plant's public address and radio systems, so I also heard the everyday comments and problems, and thereby "heard" the pulse of the operation.

During the day I spent time visiting various plant areas, and after hours I frequently walked through the plant to "sense" the pulse of the operation. The observations made from my office, however, were more revealing as to what was really going on in the plant. They also helped me focus on various problems in my daily plant strolls.

Throughout the experiment I kept a close watch for potential problems or opportunities by ascertaining people's moods, thereby "feeling" the pulse of the operation. When I intuitively felt the situation needed some extra help, I would investigate it immediately and assure *conflict control* — thereby assuring I could continue to delegate or diffuse responsibilities. Problems were not allowed to fester or get out of hand. The bells continued to ring throughout the experiment, though many continued to dislike them. They became a reminder of the whole cloth of *conflict control*.

Throughout the experiment, each individual's focus continued to be on his or her own needs, but the focus of the individual's need to belong shifted from his or her job function to his or her team and *their* plant.

Each new team was carefully structured and chartered, and each team had all of the human resources required for success. The main thrust of all of the teams was to support the operators. They played the most direct role and had the most immediate impact in controlling the volume and quality of plant output. It was, of course, the amount of enrichment we so produced that was of crucial significance to the macro organization.

It is problematic, but perhaps additional wealth through people and *conflict control* may have been created had the thrust been aimed less exclusively at operators. Our prudence allowed the experiment to survive, however, and the experiment ended before we could seriously consider this matter of thrust. Even so, some of the teams were *structured* along functional lines.

Not all of the teams included a supervisor (the area teams did not), and most teams did not have a designated leader (but all had leadership). Every individual in the plant — including the janitor and the secretary — was on at least two teams of dissimilar nature. This meant that each person had at least two vehicles through which he or she could *strive for harmonious excellence*.

Throughout the experiment, management-type powers and privileges were filtered down throughout the organization. Similarly, the union contract stipulations were bent toward flexibility. At one point, we held a series of discussions in the plant on the subject of common sense and flexibility. The practice of common sense and flexibility was thereafter encouraged but never forced.

Occasionally, external pressures from top management would force our plant to back away from a change that had been made, but we always kept striving (albeit quietly), and the change almost always eventually prevailed — often to the benefit of the other plants in the complex. Our plant went about making changes as quietly as possible so as to minimize unnecessary external disruption. Because we didn't broadcast either before or after the fact, many otherwise doomed changes were successfully executed. Our efforts to isolate ourselves as much as possible, and to persuade outsiders when we were exposed, caused us to sometimes feel like we were politicians (in the positive sense of the word).

Individuals in the plant often were involved with teams other than plant production teams. For example, I was part of a product management team whose other members represented marketing, research, and customer technical services. Our job was to develop and evolve a coordinated plan of future activities for these functions. The primary accountability of each member was to his or her parent function, rather than to the long-range goals of the team (in this particular case the goal was increased business). Such ambiguity is typical of most teams. In our case, no function achieved its goals because no meaningful cooperation occurred. Consequently, optimum creation of wealth was never achieved. Our reports hinted at problems and opportunities, and seemed to promise better future performance, but little was actually accomplished. Our real business was accomplished higher in the organization. It appeared that there was never any real determination for it to be otherwise; eventually the team was allowed to die. Had there been a focus within our team on *striving for harmonious excellence through conflict control*, we would have been vastly more successful, and the climate in which the plant's business was conducted would have been significantly more effective.

As it was, the team members played roles rather than being themselves. They avoided the voluntary commitment of themselves and their functions rather than risking any team conflict that might become visible to their bosses. There was no trust; instead, there were oblique power maneuvers to impose or block ideas subtly. The team members took solace in paper promises of profit and in superficial togetherness rather than seeking pride and dignity (and business volume) through striving for customer satisfaction. It is not intrinsic that teams behave this way, but it is not unusual. However, a team that behaves this way is not actually a team. The cause of such failure is sometimes the way the group is structured, but more often it is the way the group is chartered.

At times — but not in a team context — marketing would ask production to provide a person to accompany a salesman on a customer visit. This was usually in response to some sort of a quality problem. Such rare production visits were invariably productive in terms of customer satisfaction — not because the product always improved as a result, but because the production person's caring and professionalism increased customer trust and confidence. Even so, such displays of the basic behavior mechanism at work were never successfully transferred to the product management team itself. The connection between caring and trust did not carry over to our team. The connection between *conflict control* and *harmonious excellence* was never made.

Conflict control, though fundamentally simple and natural, is not always easy to practice, so some situations in the plant were naturally more difficult than others. In one case, a shift supervisor we'll call Joe insisted that the discipline administered by the other shift teams was not tough enough. It seemed irrelevant to him that his team's performance was not as good as the other teams. When the teams were first formed, each individual was given as much freedom as practical to choose the team he would be on, and Joe felt the other teams had better people.

All efforts made by Joe's peers and by his team members failed to help him change his perceptions of the quality of his people and the discipline administered by others. Similarly, efforts to help him identify specific plant changes that could be reversed to improve his situation also failed. Joe's only solution was for someone to force all the supervisors to see things his way — to return to the old days when the supervisor was the "boss." However, others did not consider this to be a viable solution.

Joe's visits to the industrial psychologist, which I arranged, did not reveal a way to help him adapt in his current position. The alienation he felt with his peers and the people on his shift team continued to deepen and had reached serious proportions when a supervisory job opened up in another plant — a plant that manifested a different work climate and represented the opportunity for a fresh start. After interplant managerial discussions, an interview at the other plant was arranged, and Joe then asked to make the lateral move. For a while things went well for him at the other job, but he eventually left the company.

Around the time Joe moved to the other plant, I belatedly deduced that a specific interpersonal conflict between him and me during the strike (which I had forgotten in the meantime), had been a significant cause of his problem. It naturally remained unresolved in his mind after his transfer to the other plant; therefore I had mixed feelings about Joe leaving the company. I felt the company, particularly myself, had failed to help a valuable human being give of himself, which he was able to do after he left our company and assumed a nonsupervisory career. I had kept my pledge to help anyone find another job of his choice, but this was the only instance during our entire case study where unresolved conflict continued to the degree that a person felt there was no choice but to leave the plant.

In a different case, zero defects performance for an extended period of time had been achieved for the first time in the history of our plant. Defects were the most important measure of quality performance at the time. Each of the products made in the plant was classified. If a unit of production met specifications (zero defects), it was classified as "good"; if it did not, it was classified as "bad." There was no intrinsic interest in producing and selling bad products. A fixed amount of scrap was allowed during machine start-ups and shutdowns and was not considered a defect, but this will not be a factor in our discussion.

Beyond these usual classifications, our company sold what was called "medium" products, and there was an entrenched interest in selling them. These were products that were barely bad in some minor characteristic and were not perceived as truly bad, and presumably were not perceived as a quality problem where marketed. However, they were usually sold at a lower price than the companion good products, *and* they were packaged with a name that mirrored the generic naming of bad products. All customers were aware of this practice.

A problem arose when zero defects performance dried up the inventory of medium products. I opted for some new names for these products so that they could be categorized as good on production records when that was indeed the case, thereby reflecting actual plant performance. Marketing practices would not be compromised by the new names, although our pricing policy might have to be a little more sophisticated. The product management team turned down my request, and zero defect production was simply called bad so that it could be shipped as medium.

This affected the performance of individuals in the plant who had previously achieved pride and dignity in their zero defects performance. Regrettably, there soon became available an ample supply of truly medium grade products. Trust is indeed powerful yet fragile.

I did not anticipate this result of zero defects performance soon enough. Even so, had there been enough marketing and sales understanding of the potential of *conflict control* (the true basis of the plant's zero defects performance) — had the climate in the macro organization been one of *conflict control* — then the time might have been taken by marketing and salespeople to help sell individuals in the plant on the need to call good product bad. The professional pride of the employees would have managed to elicit a more mature plant reaction than that which occurred.

Instead, there ensued the production of nonspecification products. The waste of nonspecification production did not affect customer satisfaction; but, being waste, it did affect the creation of wealth by individuals in the plant. Perhaps more effective measures of customer satisfaction and more meaningful marketing responses will help preclude such counterproductive situations in the future.

I was unable to convince the plant workers that prior outside compliments regarding their zero defects performance had not been hollow, but I successfully repaired the damaged trust within the plant. A new internal record keeping system was set up so that performance could be more easily tracked internally. It represented additional record keeping at the time, but it eventually replaced the macro organization's traditional system.

The trust of the individuals in the plant in the macro organization was repaired enough so that my efforts to increase our acceptance of marketing's perception of reality were successful. Zero defects again became the norm, but they were never again a significant source of the enthusiasm that enhances professionalism.

In another case, the shift supervisors had been delegated the responsibility of scheduling their own vacations. Short notice of intent to take vacation was permitted, but it was to occur only when absolutely necessary. Some of the supervisors perceived that two shift supervisors were abusing the intent, thereby unnecessarily disrupting the others' schedules. *Conflict control* eventually faltered in this instance.

I arranged for an after work dinner meeting for all the shift supervisors and the production function manager, whom we'll call James and who had been the shift supervisors' boss prior to the experiment — they now reported directly to me. (It should be noted that James had felt somewhat threatened by no longer being a line supervisor.) The charter of the meeting was to resolve the short-notice vacation conflict.

I had asked for a written synopsis of the meeting from each attendee. (Interestingly, the synopsis from Joe, the shift supervisor who later left the plant, was the most relevant.) Apparently, the two "sides" of shift supervisors were reluctant to have a confrontation, and it was James, the function manager, who had to trigger a meaningful discussion. It was not apparent whether the supervisors' reluctance reflected a desire to avoid conflict, or simply reflected their former relationship with the function manager, or reflected their uncertainties in their evolving roles in *conflict control*.

The consensus reached at the meeting was that mutual understanding had been achieved, and, indeed, in the litmus of time, no further conflict was obvious. The shift supervisors continued to schedule their own vacations, and the number of short notices declined somewhat. In my subsequent individual discussions with all of the meeting attendees, I was satisfied that the conflict had been resolved and not submerged. I also noticed that James, the function manager, had found more satisfaction in his leadership-by-default role than he would have in the role of boss. He was becoming more comfortable in his job.

In yet another case, an operator we'll call Ed always refused to work overtime, which put an extra burden on others. But he did have enough trust to give as much of himself as possible in order to minimize the internal conflict his overtime refusal generated. For example, he took shorter coffee breaks so others could take longer ones, and he always reported early to work so that those he relieved could have more time to prepare to leave, but he could not find a complete solution.

Ed's team members had enough trust in him to take the time to discover the reason for his refusal to work overtime. They found the reason was simply that his wife did not want him to do it. It then took them two years of helping — through social contacts such as plant safety barbecues and plant open houses — to convince her that Ed's job performance was something both he and she could be proud of, that they respected and needed him on their teams, and that his job was far more important than being merely a source of income. After that she trusted enough to allow Ed the pride and dignity of working his share of overtime; she trusted enough to sacrifice some of her much-cherished time with him. By behaving as if they existed for each other, Ed and his teammates ended two years of harmonious dedication to coping with conflict for the achievement of excellence.

RESULTS

This case study began in late 1972 and ended in 1975, although the experiment continued to mid 1977. The quantitative performance results that follow can be ascribed solely to people striving for *harmonious excellence through conflict control* because the remaining environment in which the plant operated was constant throughout the case study.

1. Plant output increased by an amount equal to one and one-half times the design capacity of the plant, and capital expenditures were only one sixth of the previous expenditures for similar output increases. Those who knew best how to keep the plant on stream and running at high rates were allowed and helped to do so — namely, the operators.
2. Zero defects were produced for over three straight weeks on two occasions near the end of the case study, in contrast to a maximum of three straight days prior to *conflict control*. Those who could best anticipate and prevent quality variance were allowed and helped to do so — namely, the operators.
3. The plant operated without downtime for over four straight weeks near the end, in contrast to four straight days previously. Those who could best anticipate and prevent mechanical problems were allowed and helped to do so — namely the craftsmen and operators.
4. Costs were $.046 per unit in contrast to $.088. This achievement reflects many results of *conflict control*, including: increased output per hour and decreased downtime, increased accountability of everyone for resource utilization, and a natural concern for waste and its attendant reduction in the cost of quality — actually, a reduction in the plant cost of lack of quality (but not including the overall cost of lack of quality to society).
5. Except for promotions and lateral moves, the turnover of people and absenteeism were zero — these are the quintessential quantitative measures of *conflict control*.
6. Safety performance was excellent. For example, there were no serious injuries throughout the case study, but this performance began evolving prior to the case study. It had been an item of special concern for the macro organization.

POSTSCRIPT

At the end of the case study, I felt that the surface of the potential of *striving for harmonious excellence through conflict control* had only been scratched. Even so, the people at the plant were the envy of the other people of the complex throughout the case study. The waiting list for hiring into our plant was always very long.

I moved to another job in mid 1977 and the experiment ended. Much of what had been started survived and continued to spread to other plants.

Pride and dignity are powerful motivators, and are essential to optimizing the creation of wealth through people. *Striving for harmonious excellence*, enhanced and optimized by *conflict control*, is the way of life required for the optimization of productivity, quality, and fulfillment. All that is required is that a simple and natural approach to leadership be allowed to help people achieve that optimization. This is what our experiment ultimately proved.

CHAPTER 3

HOW WE HAVE NOT UTILIZED HUMAN RESOURCES

To understand what we Americans are doing wrong in management begins with the recognition of two human longings discussed in detail in CHAPTER ONE, UNDERLYING RATIONALE OF HOW WEALTH IS CREATED: the longing for contentment and fulfillment. It must be recognized that we have exploited the former and stifled the latter, and that we are unfortunately continuing this practice. Some basic misconceptions of people account for our continuing dilemma.

THE BASIC MISCONCEPTION

Exploiting contentment and stifling fulfillment in people does not reflect any inherent consequence of the free enterprise philosophy or its symbol: profits. Rather, it reflects the fact that American managers have not yet utilized the real source of the tremendous potential of people. (We have also failed to accomplish it outside the economic realm.) This is our basic management flaw. It stems to a significant degree from our passion for managing our institutions by control of only measurable performance and from not foreseeing that this evolves into self-defeating views of jobs, people, and leadership. Our management focus on quantitative measures *has* led to successful management of our physical, technological, and financial resources; but that focus has failed us in management of our people resources.

There is nothing wrong with trying to measure and control to improve profits, cash flow, production output, prices, and inventory in daily business operations. There is also nothing wrong with trying to measure or improve people performance; it is when we try to control behavior through quantitative measures that we are mistaken. The attempt to control people's behavior in the interest of performance and profit predictability is understandable, but foolish because it ignores the reality of basic human motivation.

The best that can be achieved when we limit ourselves to behavior control is for only measurable factors to respond predictably (and perhaps to improve as long as pressure is applied), i.e., absenteeism, injury rate, and output per person. However, a work climate such as this diminishes the creation of wealth through people because it is based on externally imposed fear as previously noted. That, coupled with the reality that quantitative measures do not measure real people productivity, results in meaningless (and hence, misleading) cause and effect conclusions regarding productivity and profit.

Having misled ourselves, we have proceeded to draw other conclusions, such as: the work ethic is dead, or the more general conclusion, that we have lost our drive. The work ethic (work for the sake of work and because it is right and satisfying) never really existed, but something akin to it did exist — the ethic that striving for pride and dignity will ultimately lead to achievement. This ethic, although not articulated as such, was once a feature of our society; it was supported by America's hope for the future and the certitude of the belief that achievement for the "greater good" was right. The *apparent* demise of this work ethic was caused by many complex situations.

For example, we have been stifled by the dehumanizing effects of increased complexity in managing our ever-more-massive institutions. We have learned through education and experience that the rest of the world doesn't march to the same drummer as we do, and that we cannot isolate ourselves from that world — a world which is, nevertheless, foreign to our heritage. Our bonds of ethnic security and family solidarity have been stretched to the breaking point: In countless ways we have been shocked into uncertainty. This has led us to look inward in our quest for fulfillment and has blurred our understanding of how to achieve our destiny (which we can do only through and with others), and our hope has consequently been ravaged.

Increased knowledge and business sophistication account for much of the decrease of our pride and dignity ethic. Americans learned more about how business institutions function and how they change over the years as they grow and expand. It eventually became apparent that we erred when we assumed our institutions were the wellspring of our justification for our hope and certitude. Apparently, all of our institutions (industry, commerce, government, education, finance, and religion) carved out different management styles and niches of activity for themselves as society became more complex. Adversarialism grew among the institutions and within their various departments as management turf was fiercely defended from within the walls that had been erected. It is in the gaps between those walls that many of the aspirations and hopes of Americans have been lost.

It is not that our institutions cannot inspire people; it is just that they fail to do so, or fail to follow through. As long as the noted adversarialism exists, our institutions apparently will be unable to help a person to pursue his or her individual destiny. Fortunately, our institutions have been unable to cause our humanness to completely disappear; *some* fulfillment can still be found in our everyday lives outside our institutions.

Even though our institutions may never serve the needs of the whole person, there is a way in which they can be less of a hindrance while they otherwise continue to serve their purposes admirably. Our institutions should allow, rather than prevent, people to tap on their own, and with the help of others, the true source of their aspirations. Our institutions should allow them to find as much self-fulfillment and productivity as they possibly can by letting their free will meet the demands of the spirit while on the job. As in the case study, this *will* improve productivity and fulfillment, and success will breed success. It is not inconceivable that this could eventually lead to our finding practical ways for our institutions to cooperate with each other for our greater common good.

Some evidence exists that this can happen. For example, in Japan, when one corporation buys from another, there are many instances of the buyer using essentially zero inspection (and hence, zero inspection cost) on a routine basis when purchasing material. This is the result of the supplier's established trustworthiness that its material will satisfy the buyer; this is precisely the same trust that is integral to *conflict control*.

Our failure to grasp the concept that the fulfillment of individuals while at work will improve the productivity and quality of the corporation is not due solely to our passion for measurement. Another cause is one of our deeply ingrained, but nevertheless superficial, mores. It has to do with the nature of the real world.

THE REAL WORLD

That Americans are not yet heading in the right direction as a people, and that our lack of understanding of people still characterizes us, are reflections of the difference in what people think is the real world and what the real world actually is. It begins with our sense perceptions and judgments: The weather is hot. Our profits are low. He is walking slowly. We then proceed to classify the object perceived: The desert is inhospitable. The competitor's pricing is outrageous. He is lazy. Most classifications are flawed since they result quickly from initial observations. They are nevertheless a real force that continues to linger even after a more thorough analysis is made; they constitute what people perceive as the real world.

Classifications simply evaluate the relationship of what we sense to our personal values expressed in terms of expectations, norms, hopes, or desires. Since our values seem immutable to us, when challenged we tend to preserve them by intensely justifying and defending our classifications. This, of course, does not sit well with those whom we classify. To expect others to behave in accordance with our personal values is irrational. When we attempt to force our values on their behavior, we instead intensify adversarialism.

Yet people's values do differ. The question remains as to how such differences can realistically be accommodated since we cannot expect others to voluntarily accept our values. In the real world, however, it is rational and possible to sidestep values and concentrate instead on *right* (i.e., concentrate instead on the reality of being human) in a trusting quest for the mutual satisfaction of needs.

In the real world, it is understood that behavior sensed by others is the result of heredity, knowledge, experience, circumstances, and the work climate — behavior control versus *conflict control*, distrust versus trust. Except for heredity, the manager of a group of people has some influence over these various factors, and in the factor of work climate he or she essentially has absolute control in a behavior control climate. The *manager's* experience, observations, values, and needs determine the work climate in a behavior control climate. Since such a boss must control people's behavior, it behooves him or her to prevent behavior surprise since surprise is the antithesis of control. Such prevention is always expected and must be produced if the boss is to survive and prosper.

The boss must also fine-tune the use of the other resources at his or her disposal (money, tools, organization, etc.) in the interest of profits while also satisfying (in the interest of his or her career) the other expectations his or her superior may have at any particular moment in time. Being this sort of boss is not easy, and it becomes more difficult as behavior control must be continuously reinforced if surprises are to be prevented. Any desire the boss may have to be trusted by his or her people by helping them on their terms will be submerged, along with other needs (the boss' own fulfillment, for example) that the *false* real world disallows.

In submerging such needs, the boss is failing to deal with reality (just as his or her superior is), because the true real world must accommodate other people's personal values and longings for fulfillment which cannot be diminished even when stifled. In denying his or her own need for fulfillment, the boss further embeds his or her distorted values; the boss' discord and insecurity increase, and his or her values become more distorted, as the boss vainly struggles to justify them.

The most rational explanation of such a situation is greed. The greed for power over others as an end in itself, as self-justification, or as a way to make money. As greed feeds on itself, it prevents the boss from finding trust enough to grow; the increasing discord in the boss' mind renders the justification of his or her behavior even more irrational. It is not that the boss is intrinsically more greedy than others; it is simply that, for whatever reasons, the boss is in a position with which he or she has not yet been able to rationally cope.

If the boss' greed does yield the power he or she seeks, the boss' destiny is foreclosed as his perceptions of reality become more distorted. He or she also disallows people from pursuing their own destinies as he or she imposes more behavior control while trying to satisfy a personal longing for contentment through the status quo. The boss' greed-driven desire for power and recognition increasingly whets his or her appetite for controlling people through fear, which contrasts with a *leader* who, in desiring growth, increasingly whets his or her appetite for helping people to trust.

Beyond the consequences of imposed fear, the behavior control boss compounds his or her problem when his or her personal values and style are the standards against which people are classified. If the boss communicates this to the people involved, he or she assures the highest possible degree of people's distrust and adversarialism. People become polarized against their boss and against management in general.

In this regard, he or she seems to be defied most often by the 5 percent or so of employees who appear to be misfits — who almost always seem to be counterproductive in any society. They usually trigger the imposition of additional behavior control (on everyone, of course) because threats of job security or job termination do not induce fear and behavior conformity in them.

In contrast, in a *conflict control* climate the 5 percent are helped by others. In the case study (except for the supervisor who left his job), the 5 percent did "disappear" since they were not a fixed group in a static control system, but rather an ever-changing group in a dynamic growth system.

It is not likely the distortion called the real world is going to disappear of its own volition. That people may decide individually to rectify it, as in the case study, is nevertheless a possibility. One must wonder what the real bottom line might be if the distortion called the real world continues unabated as the dominant management characteristic of our society. It may very well so continue since it is not easy for a manager to escape the behavior control trap. If individual efforts fail to rectify the trend, one must wonder what, if anything, can accomplish it. In fact, one must wonder if our institutions have already gone along the wrong path of people management to a point where no one is held accountable for it — to a point of no return.

ACCOUNTABILITY

The boss has a boss who has a boss! This continues upward through the hierarchy until the top boss is reached — and along the way accountability gets diffused in a behavior control climate. When the top boss is involved in the workings of the line organization in such a climate, it is unrealistic to assume that the basic misconception of human needs will disappear on its own because the top boss is subjected to the mishandling of needs by many management layers, and he or she must struggle to impose any type of change at the bottom successfully. In fact, it is unlikely that misconceptions can be prevented from deepening in a large organization as long as the top boss in a behavior control climate is actively involved in the line hierarchy; there may simply be too many layers of misguided managers for realism to escape being smothered to death.

Nevertheless, if *conflict control* is to replace behavior control and optimize the creation of wealth through people — if *conflict control* is to replace profit as *the* societal value of an organization — then someone, somewhere in the organization must assume the risk of making it happen, because behavior control feeds on itself.

Let's hypothesize that the priority of the top boss' values changes, for example, and that he or she decides to implant *conflict control*. Even if the top boss could then induce one of his or her managers to start the process, neither the top boss nor the manager is likely to "find" the time (as opposed to "taking" the time) required to convince multiple layers of management to meaningfully support the manager to the extent that *conflict control* will successfully be implanted at the bottom.

As an alternative (one of many), the top boss can start with his or her staff and then try to assure that it somehow trickles down. Unfortunately for this approach, *conflict control* cannot occur overnight and cannot be the direct result of corporate edict (trust is not enhanced by edicts). It would be unpredictable in terms of timing, and any problematic effects of this approach (such as interpersonal conflict), viewed later out of context, could be perceived as undesirable by inexperienced managers. Consequently, given the ingrained values of behavior control bosses, the practice of *conflict control* would probably take what might well be perceived as an excessive amount of time for its benefits to trickle down through, and to survive, the layers of negative viewpoints.

In pursuing *conflict control*, sufficient trust is either built or not built. For a trickle-down approach to be successful, we must presuppose that building trust can begin at the upper echelons where, as it has been shown, its value has probably been distorted (albeit unintentionally, perhaps). Large organizations therefore are less likely than smaller organizations to switch to *conflict control* deliberately. Nevertheless, *conflict control* can start anywhere in any organization as long as there is sufficient opportunity, as well as understanding, desire, and will. Thus, the difficulties of the top boss in a large organization operating in a behavior control climate do not render him or her any less accountable for his or her situation, in spite of perceptions, hopes, opinions, arguments, or golden parachutes to the contrary. If the top boss, representing the owners in managing the organization for their profit, is not accountable for people's performance, then it is not rational to presume that anyone else can be accountable.

This is not to say that the top boss' performance is not proscribed by corporate geopolitics, changing demographics, various cartels and other macro conditions over which he or she does not have complete control (but the effects of these conditions can at least be anticipated). Regardless, the accountability for the insidiousness of further entrenchment by behavior control as the essence of misunderstanding is ultimately the top boss'. The rules enforcer *is* ultimately accountable for the behavior of all of the players.

Perhaps this intrinsic accountability of the top boss is why most proposed programs for improving productivity and quality, according to their own hype, must begin at the executive level. Given the apparent unwillingness of owners to hold top management accountable for optimizing employee performance, it is ironic that at the outset these programs impede the very success they seek. The behavior mechanism *is* immutable, but oblique thrusts aimed at some aspects of it cannot significantly blunt the insidiousness of behavior control; only the frontal attack of *conflict control* can do that.

PRODUCTIVITY PROGRAMS

There are countless programs available to managers who want to improve the productivity of their operation, but behavior controls circumvent the potential of all such plans. Historically, most support and implementation have begun at top management levels. When these programs so benefit from executive interest, they suffer from the trickle-down effect; when there is executive disinterest, they benefit from a relatively pure application of their principles at the lower level, but they suffer from a lack of support. Because the programs are subjected to these limitations, and because their universality is proscribed by their own detailed, step-by-step narrow approaches, they are at best minimally successful. Productivity programs further suffer from management's unrealistic expectation that people will readily accept them and will readily allow themselves to be separated from the secure contentment of detailed job limits and the security of the invisible job walls thereby created.

Along with the time that is required to successfully encourage *conflict control* in people lies the ever-present arbitrary time frame (for producing results) that is so much a facet of a behavior control climate. In retrospect, the enthusiastic beginning of a participative management program — the enthusiasm that accompanies participation — is doomed to disappear, because the boss in a behavior control climate will continue to decide who will make which decisions. For similar reasons, a program such as bottoms-up management cannot even get started because it would be perceived as an obvious contradiction of terms since the boss at the outset would arbitrarily decide if and when "top down" should supplant "bottom up" which, of course, it must from time to time.

Programs such as quality circles apply universal, how-to details for identifying and solving group problems and appear to be more universally applicable than do some of the other programs. Even so, those very details result in the perception that they need to be practiced in only a few of the dynamic and complex relationships of any group's endeavor. In quality circles, the relationship is a group meeting away from each person's job site. That relationship is quite similar to the area teams in the case study except that it does not accommodate unspecified tasks — namely, how it is that *that* group will become a team. It may be taken for granted that the transformation to a real team will occur naturally, but it is an unrealistic presumption — especially if profit is the bottom line of the group effort (which it usually is).

In contrast, such programs can succeed in a *conflict control* climate anywhere they are meaningfully applicable, because none of the implementation obstacles are factors in its ultimate success (other than the program's built-in details, which will eventually be accepted for what they should be — guidelines for success rather than stipulations of additional behavior control).

One of the many programs in current vogue is statistical quality control (sometimes called statistical process control), and its foremost proponent is W. Edwards Deming, whose accomplishments in quality control are universally acclaimed. In the interest of detecting *significant* variability of process performance, it simply specifies what information is to be gathered, how it is to be organized, and how it is to be presented, thereby giving direction to any required corrective actions. It is unique in that it focuses on significant process variability rather than directly on profit performance or behavior control.

Statistical quality control (SQC) has not been widely applied in America as a mathematical tool even though it was developed here in the 1920s. Statistics did find some application, however, in presenting variations (in time) of quality parameters with respect to their standards or specifications. It was occasionally used to help management decide when to take corrective action, but usually it was used only to report quality status.

In SQC's present form, comparison to a standard as its basic output is disallowed. Instead, the information gathered is to be used to decide if action should be taken based only on the degree of variation itself. With the use of any additional relevant information, it is then decided how to reduce the variability. In this sense, SQC is a realistic concept: Its philosophy supports the reduction of variability (waste) simply for the sake of reducing it, thus lowering cost and significantly improving quality.

The use of this approach in America is growing, but is not yet widespread. Selected portions of it are more widely practiced, but in themselves are not evidence of its intrinsic validity and may tend to mask its true strength. Generally, its use simply evidences its appeal to people with a passion for quantitative measures. So far, the statistical measures and the control charts seem to be the most popular portions.

Some authorities, especially Deming, who have nurtured the acceptance of SQC have stipulated that to achieve its full creative potential, its serious practice must go beyond statistical mental discipline and its attendant how-to details. SQC must also include ideas such as elimination of people's fear, discouragement of quantitative measurements of the performance of people, and stimulation of constant change. These ideas clearly indicate compatibility with the concept of *conflict control* because creativity is encouraged, and direct control of behavior with edicts is discouraged.

Proponents further suggest that when embracing these SQC ideas, the practice will eventually lead to realization of its full potential. One of their observations is that 85 percent of the detected variability will be ascribable to the system and 15 percent to the people who perform the operation. If everyone involved were to meaningfully contribute to remedying the 85 percent and the 15 percent variabilities, then the creativity and dedication that is required to find the best solutions might be achieved. Again, success would tend to breed success. This leads precisely to the problem that presents itself in a behavior control climate — few involved people are actually going to contribute to the solution because it will have been imposed by the boss, and only by sheer accident will it have been the best solution.

The 85 percent variability answer does not lie with management alone. Who better than those who have been subjected to mismanagement might know what problems caused it? Similarly, for the 15 percent variability, what other than leadership can help the responsible person develop and implement a good solution?

Even if the people who perform that operation receive external help (such as training) to improve their job skills, or to discover some other way to improve their overall group variability, the solutions, whatever their source, will not have been optimized in a behavior control climate. They will not have resulted from the creativity of people giving of themselves completely.

Beyond proscribing meaningful solutions, the future success of the longing for fulfillment will not have been enhanced. Any skill training provided will be perceived merely as a form of manipulation in the interest of profit, and will not stimulate future self-motivation. Such training, however, will be accepted and utilized because it *will* be perceived by an individual as having enhanced his or her future financial security. Thus, practice of SQC in a behavior control climate does not guarantee the adoption of the concepts that are required for full development of SQC potential, for the climate disallows the intuition required to utilize fully the possible solutions to detected variability. Quite the opposite is true in a *conflict control* climate.

The negative effects of a behavior control, greed-producing climate on management programs seems obvious. Yet, many are surprised that focusing on the quantifiable elements of profits dooms productivity programs; it is nevertheless irrational to be surprised that those who are not directly accountable for profits per se are not self-motivated by profits.

Most people in a company can directly influence only a few quantitative elements of profit, i.e., a product's raw material cost, labor cost, or sales income. It is not likely that any person will feel sufficient responsibility for profit when he or she has such little impact. When an individual does not believe that his or her contribution is recognizably meaningful to management, he or she will not feel any accountability. It is unrealistic for management to expect people to relate to corporate profits unless their personal impact on these profits can be made clear to them and is clearly appreciated by management. This may not be possible.

The problem of employees not relating to profits is fundamental. It is rooted in the very nature of profit, since profit is measured in terms of a quantity of money, and money is perceived as being neither good nor bad. The concept of money is conceived in the mind as an abstract symbol, while the concept of creativity, in contrast, is conceived as a concrete vision. Dollar profits in themselves will not stimulate employee enthusiasm, but job creativity will. Money itself is uninspiring until it is in the possession of one who can spend it. On the other hand, the opportunity to give of one's self is inspiring and will result in creativity and productivity. Therefore, corporate profits do not directly stimulate motivation in employees who do not directly benefit from them. Thus, no meaningful "profit-personal growth" relationships exist for most people. It cannot be expected that most people will believe that such relationships may ever exist for them.

It is not that the concept of profits and their economic validity is not well understood, nor is it that the relationship of profits to job security is not perfectly understood. It is that amoral concepts cannot be perceived as inherently *right* and nothing, not even externally imposed fear, can change this.

Although dollar profits do not motivate people, *how* the profits are achieved might motivate them since this is not perceived as amoral. How profits are achieved in a behavior control climate, (i.e., through control of behavior) is demotivating.

OTHER APPROACHES

Beyond programs, other attempts are made to improve quantified measures of productivity in the interest of profits. Profit sharing is one such approach. In this plan people, through the greed induced by their behavior control environment, will respond favorably to increasing profits because it represents financial gain. But pride and dignity do not accompany this greed. If profits decrease people respond negatively, and their stifled longing for job fulfillment will be displaced by a longing for contentment. The bottom line will be heightened insecurity and, consequently, a decrease in productivity.

Modifications to profit-sharing plans (such as a five-year trailing average) may reduce some of the self-defeating excesses of profit cycle upswings. For example, greed may result in equipment abuse; with a dampened profit cycle, greed, and hence equipment abuse, might also be dampened.

In contrast, greed is perceived as an incorrect need in a *conflict control* climate, and is therefore less prevalent; with profit-sharing modifications, it might even be completely mitigated.

Another approach, particularly with newly formed companies, is to select as employees only those people who already think and behave as the boss requires. At this point behavior control has not yet set in because the boss' expectations justify their personal values and styles and therefore they willingly comply. Profit sharing is often a feature of this approach. Since profits begin at a low level in most new companies, profit sharing will appear to enhance performance during the initial period of operations.

However, except in a behavior control climate where people's insecurity increases, people grow and their needs change; they acquire knowledge and experience over time. Similarly, the needs of the corporation change as it matures. Disparities in the needs between an individual and a group, and among individuals, will develop. In the absence of *conflict control*, these differences will assure that behavior control and adversarialism and greed will eventually predominate human relationships. When profits decline the situation is more severe. The result is inexorably the same, even if the people themselves own the business.

The substitution of computers for people is also another attempt to improve productivity. Computers are marvelous and exciting. They have almost unlimited potential for improving our personal lives and our work tasks, and we have probably barely realized the universality of their applications. Computers eliminate drudgery in tasks such as designing robotics and data handling. They allow us to better visualize spatial relationships and understand cause and effect relationships. They may someday be capable of demonstrating the counter-productivity of a behavior control climate, and of proving that *conflict control* optimizes wealth and profits. Behavior control, however, is not likely to be the climate in which such proof will be either sought or accepted.

At their current stage of evolution, computers have serious drawbacks as replacements for people. One problem is a degree of inflexibility, since computer updating tends to be costly as knowledge expands and needs change. They tend to lock present "truths" into future objectives. As replacements for people they are so far incapable of creativity; thus it is ironic that such quantitative output is sometimes used to justify replacing people. It is nevertheless inevitable that this will happen in businesses that pay attention to only quantitatively measured performance.

The difficulties in updating computers as changes occur cause additional insecurity in the remaining people unless they mitigate it by satisfying other needs. Their need to give of themselves cannot be satisfied by a computer system since it is incapable of communicating with their human needs. They can mitigate the insecurity generated in them by the computer in effect having replaced people only if they are operating in a *conflict control* climate.

Regarding communicating with human needs, computers might be able to serve productively as an ancillary communication system in a Job Scope type of organization with its clearly defined areas of interest and accountability. Such a system would be designed to provide information about what is happening in other areas of the endeavor. This would be nonroutine information such as recent glitches and successes of the endeavor and the people who populate it, entered by those to whom it happened.

Briefly, the lack of computer creativity seems obvious in its implications, but naturally is not perceived as a problem in a behavior control climate where creativity is not valued and seldom occurs.

Computers may not *truly* solve any problems if people are replaced without regard for implications such as in a behavior control climate. For example, an overstaffed organization will probably simply overcomputerize as it replaces people, not realistically foreseeing computer expense, downtime, inflexibility, maintenance, and obsolescence. Computerization does not cure mismanagement. Further, there are costs to society that are not accounted for by the internal decision to let people go. Other institutions, with their narrow foci in terms of their missions, are ill-equipped to effectively help the displaced people survive, much less utilize their talents, and the productivity of our nation receives yet another blow.

Mergers and acquisitions are yet another means used by corporations to increase productivity and profits. When the strengths of the individual companies complement one another, the use of this approach may be fully justified. Even so, the benefits to our nation can only be hoped for because of the present difficulty of measuring any societal implications.

For example, a number of people usually are let go after a corporate merger. As in the case of computers displacing people, talents and skills are usually squandered, and no other corporation or institution (government, education, religion, etc.) conceives of taking the initiative in redirecting these talents and skills as part of its mission; and government welfare (although aimed at a worthwhile cause doesn't improve the nation's productivity) is all that prevents disaster for many of the displaced.

Unfortunately, the decision of companies to merge is sometimes miscalculated; the advantages of combined corporate incomes, expenditures, and profits are overestimated in behavior control climates. For example, the savings in salaries is apt to be lower than expected; the new, larger organization probably will need more than the projected number of people to force behavior to produce the predicted results.

Accompanying this situation, people at the bottom of the hierarchy in a behavior control environment will perceive those at the top to have lost another opportunity for improving the climate because of greed (in this instance the greed of short-term profits in the absence of leadership of people). They will realize that many of the corporate merger goals could have been met without merging had only people's creativity and dedication been unleashed previously. They end up feeling more like bonded servants and less like important contributors to the new company's destiny. Their productivity will decline.

The problem is not that people won't continue to conform, and try to do what is expected of them. They will try to do exactly what they believe they are paid to do, in the interest of job security. Indeed, they will try to do more if they can, but their proscribing job box will disallow this and their resulting unresolved conflict will cause a reduction in productivity. The boss, of course, will look for the people to exhibit the same attributes that the boss perceives in himself or herself, hoping for creativity and dedication in their behavior as a result of this new job security threat. Because the boss will not be able to mandate this, his or her taste for behavior control will be reinforced — thereby hastening its inevitable consequences (the boss reinforcing their longing for contentment as he or she further disallows their longing for fulfillment).

The boss may even manipulate a concept that people believe to be *right* and turn it against them. The boss may exhort, for example, "a day's work for a day's pay." But if they are already doing all they can under the circumstances, this sloganeering will simply increase their insecurity. The boss will have succeeded in deepening people's *apparent* submission, but at the price of intensifying his or her personal insecurity by denying his or her need to help others to grow through creativity, dedication, etc.

The boss may even be patronizing to the people as his or her lever of insecurity and fear is wielded by complimenting them when they do what he or she tells them to do, by inquiring about their families, by getting the water cooler fixed, etc. They will nevertheless continue to perceive that their longing for fulfillment and satisfaction is of paramount importance to them, and that their boss' irrational actions have denied this in the interest of greed. No amount of patronization will be able to alter their perceptions. In fact, patronization renders the boss' behavior control more personal and introduces a whole new set of emotional parameters to the people's sources of insecurity.

In contrast, when the corporate merger is perceived by people in a *conflict control* climate to have true potential for increasing quality and productivity, and for cooperatively producing enrichment, they will accept the decision, embrace it, and strive for its success. They will do this because their work environment is open, trusting, and creative — as in the case study where five areas were reorganized into four.

TRADITIONS

Some of our American traditions contribute to our basic management misconception and, indeed, may be a product of it. One such tradition is that people work at work, have fun away from work, relate to the spirit at a place of their choosing — but certainly not at work. Put another way, people are supposed to compartmentalize their lives.

The compartmentalizing tradition is intrinsically alien to the concept of fulfillment at work. Continuing efforts to differentiate between the quality of life and the quality of work life attest to the tenacity of this tradition, as do the ever-enlarging, dehumanizing, uncivilizing gaps between institutions.

Another such tradition is the belief that the manager's primary responsibility is concern for the owner's profits. This was probably started by the original American entrepreneurs who may have insisted on this from their hired managers. The manager's primary responsibility was not to the people who ultimately assured these profits. Given the longevity of this facet of our misunderstanding, it should not be too surprising that managers may find it justifiable to behave irrationally — including acquiescing to the misconception that power and greed are more powerful motivators than pride and dignity.

In fact, behavior control managers traditionally behave as if *they* own the company, and as if power is more important to them than their own and their people's pride and dignity. They usually react to problems within their realm of responsibility as if their people, and not they, are to blame. They sometimes behave as if harshness with their people merits special praise as a solution to their problems. This tragically growing distortion of reality epitomizes foolishness and arrogance in management whenever and wherever it exists. The prerogatives of "owners" are indeed powerful, and can be disastrous if misused.

Greed, or even fear, could explain the inception of these traditions, but what explains their continuing dominance? The most probable answer aside from greed or fear is habit, the unthinking continuation of mores, such as the traditions just noted, that are alien to American heritage. Our heritage is the pursuit by each person of his or her destiny, which requires *striving for harmonious excellence*. This can be done only by the whole person and it involves vastly more than profits. The counterproductive traditions just noted are traditions, and are not our heritage. We must break the habit of honoring them.

The solution to the dominance of this habit is the practice of *conflict control*, which would reveal the counterproductive nature of these traditions, and also would lead to their eventual demise. This would happen because in a *conflict control* climate (where people are encouraged to reason) someone will see the irrationality of such traditions, and being encouraged to self-expression will articulate this observation. Others will agree and this tradition will be discarded in their area.

Growth-stunting habits *can* be broken if a person's free will is enabled to trust enough that he or she heeds the demands of the spirit. This is facilitated if a person's conscious mind can understand the true nature of his or her discontentment. For example, in the case study the operator who designed and installed the new piping in the plant had been frustrated in previous cases by not really feeling free to express his feelings about technical people's solutions to mechanical design problems. The tradition was that only technical people solved those problems, and this seemed to work — after all, the plant was making a profit. He had subconsciously known all along that some of his ideas were more workable than theirs. After *conflict control* took root, he dared to actually believe his ideas were better, he dared to ask to be accountable for them, and management dared to let him.

These traditions may continue to flourish partly because of a void of comprehension. This void is caused by the difficulty of understanding the complex and perplexing, but nonetheless inspiring, dictum of "all men are created equal." *Conflict control* can rely on its concept of how people are alike (equal) in order to replace our un-American traditions with the *essence* of that dictum and with what *is* true to American heritage.

SUMMARY

American mismanagement of people stems from our passion for quantitatively measuring and controlling behavior. The focus of this passion — profits — leads to management's exploiting people's longing for contentment and stifling their longing for fulfillment in the interest of behavior predictability. The resulting counterproductive form of competitiveness characterizes our interinstitutional relationships as well as our interpersonal relationships.

This misconception of the real world represents alienation from the real strength of people, which is their personal growth process and destiny pursuit. This alienation feeds on itself. As we become increasingly unrealistic in our management of people, we seem to also lose our sense of our accountability. We may even lose our ability to make meaningful, positive, realistic changes in our workplace.

Programs designed for change and progress through people instead get inundated by misconceptions of the real world. This is because such programs mistakenly focus on improving dollar profits — thus nurturing our basic misconception of people — rather than on the creation of wealth. They also focus on few of the many factors involved. Yet they nevertheless contain too many how-to verities to be universally applicable.

Other approaches, such as computers, mergers, etc., are similarly unrealistic, and are similarly inundated when they occur in a behavior control climate. Some profit-oriented traditions further distort reality and erode the potential productivity achievements of people.

CHAPTER 4

HOW AND WHERE TO FULLY UTILIZE PEOPLE

The solution to our dilemma begins with our understanding that the full utilization of people as resources in the workplace requires the realization that exploiting their longing for contentment is counterproductive and that nurturing their longing for fulfillment is crucial. This is one facet of a work environment in which people are *striving for harmonious excellence* through a climate of *conflict control*. That climate, which assures the optimization of the creation of wealth through people, is the basic answer to our dilemma.

It is helpful to understand the essence of our rights as human beings. We Americans err when we focus on our "inalienable rights" and our Bill of Rights by passing laws, regulations, rules, etc., to enforce these rights. This is especially true when that focus produces laws, etc., that are quite detailed in their behavior control (which most are). The behavior mechanism inevitably causes such control to fail to deliver the intended fulfillment. Prohibition and school busing are but two examples of our many failures.

Our viewpoint of rights is also flawed because, in pursuing those rights, we seem to give little thought to the obligations those rights entail. Here again we ignore the behavior mechanism. The behavior mechanism implies that all human beings have only one inherent right — the right to trust (which is reflected in the statement of trust that is stamped on American coins), the right to have the opportunity to give of their whole selves. It also implies that all human beings have only one inherent obligation — the obligation to seek fulfillment, the obligation to give of their whole selves.

It is on that right and that obligation that we Americans must focus, remembering that success lies in the give and take of the microprocess of *conflict control*.

Our American heritage can be of enormous help to us, but the other rights and obligations implied in that heritage must not become a primary focus of our living — they must remain what they were intended to be, i.e., simply goals toward which each of us must and can confidently strive while seeking his or her destiny.

This segment will revolve around the steps that are involved for managers who want to nurture people's longing for fulfillment, thus helping build a climate of *conflict control* through leadership. This will be a general discussion, because no detailed "how-to" instructions exist to help you develop the necessary instincts to use this approach. I have developed some insights that can assist you. The manner in which you ultimately use them will depend on some important factors: your particular workplace and its management practices, specific departmental or task requirements, and unforeseeable, but influencing, circumstances. The most important parameters, though, will be your personal experience, your psychological make-up, and your cultural background. While these parameters will determine how you use the guidelines, only your desire will ultimately determine your success.

HOW TO START IT

A manager starts this approach because he or she is told to, is inspired to, or wants to, but success depends on wanting to — feeling the *need* to help people tap their own inner strengths and talents in job performance. When I was a plant manager, I started because I was inspired by a program of my general manager and wanted to implement the program in my area. The general manager had introduced the concept of "whole job" to our company. He defined this as "a job where an individual is allowed to plan-do-evaluate."

I was not successful in moving this concept down through the management hierarchy in my plant. I eventually abandoned this definition and broadened the concept: "A whole job is any job in an environment that encourages a person to extend himself or herself — through the involvement of his or her conscience, instincts, and intellect — toward achieving meaningful, obtainable goals for the sake of his or her own dignity." This broadened concept eventually led to my concepts of *conflict control* and *harmonious excellence*, through countless evolutions of planning-doing-evaluating my new approach to leading people. Nonetheless, in retrospect, my serious consideration of rectifying plant management's misunderstanding of people *had* been *catalyzed* by the general manager.

All this predated the strike noted in the case study. I had a long-standing, strong desire to start, but it remained in the back of my mind because of the demands of my duties, the limited success of my prior attempts at change, and my fear that something so different might not be perceived by top management as compatible with the present practices in our successful profit-making endeavor.

Later, I was able to express that my desire reflected a need to lead, not merely to manage. I realized that the stronger one's desire is to reject intuition and to focus only on objective evidence, the more suppressed will be the need to lead. However, regardless of job status or social position, everyone has a need to lead by helping others to grow, and this need to lead *will* surface for attention from time to time.

The rejection of the need to help is one of the consequences of a behavior control climate. Consequently, the universality of this need is masked by the perception that people behave as if they have no need to lead, and that they want to be left alone to do only the job they are paid to do in the exact way they are paid to do it. Except for their inability to resolve ambiguities of job expectations, people in a behavior control climate do behave exactly as the boss wants them to behave. They, in effect, are heeding their longing for contentment; the boss, in effect, is exploiting that longing; through necessity, the people are denying themselves the benefits of the longing for fulfillment.

When the initial effort is made in a behavior control climate to nurture people's longing for fulfillment it is seemingly rejected. One is faced with a void of interest — no one responds at first; no visible changes in attitude or behavior occur. As efforts are continued, people slowly begin to respond. At first, individuals may ask for the satisfaction of some of their selfish personal needs — i.e., often they will want you to make others conform to their view of *right*. Because sufficient trust has not yet been established, their behavior will not yet result in job pride and dignity. It may even seem to be counterproductive or even chaotic.

For example, the proposed shift change in the case study produced, in order, disbelief (and wonder), anger (and gratitude), organized resistance (and support), despair (and hope), resignation (and persuasion). It severely polarized the group, and diverted some attention from operating the plant right up to the moment I made the decision to switch to the proposed schedule. My efforts to "sell" the new schedule continued, and the negative reactions then quickly disappeared, especially after the promised benefits actually materialized. If you mean to succeed, however, you must try to build mutual trust in spite of initial reactions that often will seem childish to you as your people test your intentions. This will be only the first of many apparent rejections that you will encounter as you build a solid base of trust.

The surest way to convince yourself that *conflict control* can't work is to expect it to produce dramatic results in its beginning stages, and to convince yourself that your people's rebuffs prove the point. Immediate improvement is an unrealistic expectation, easily producing fear and guilt in you for risking profits.

To begin the project with fanfare *invites* failure. Fanfare produces a faint hope that something good might happen; that hope will soon be more than offset by the skeptical belief that it is just another profit-driven, behavior control manipulation. Faint hope will cause fanfare to result only in elevated insecurity and increased counterproductive behavior — *conflict control* takes time to implant.

Conflict control will most certainly fail in the early stages of implementation if the accompanying increase in counterproductive behavior is ignored, however it is caused. Overlooking this problem, in the absence of a solid base of trust, *will* cause a tendency toward anarchy; it will *not* demonstrate determination to help people find self-fulfillment. At that juncture, it must be conveyed that, even though behavior will no longer be prescribed, counterproductive behavior doesn't produce job pride and personal dignity. It must be conveyed to your people that they nevertheless continue to be trusted to pursue meaningful behavior instead. Some people will then respond successfully on their own; some will respond with help; some will not respond at all.

It is at this point that the process of building trust has visibly begun, regardless of the specific techniques used to nurture the longing for fulfillment. Some effective techniques include: private conversations, fewer behavior controls, and beneficial changes — do whatever you believe to be *right* and feasible for your group of people. Sooner or later, specific changes in the work environment — something other than just talk — will need to be adopted to promote trust and growth. Both big and little changes, like those mentioned in the case study (shift change, operating teams, area teams, tool accountability, ordering of supplies, etc.) will probably be required.

In assuring that changes are made, their frequency also must be considered. Changes that occur too infrequently will encourage attempts to satisfy the longing for contentment, while changes that occur too frequently will not allow the conflict of change to be coped with, thereby increasing insecurity.

For example, had the change in shift schedule not been followed by other changes, those who perceived the least benefit from that change — having nothing else to challenge their longing for contentment, and having not been overwhelmingly fulfilled — would eventually focus on their longing for contentment, and thereby would begin to become less productive. Eventually, everyone may have fallen into this trap. On the other hand, if the concept of the operating team had been introduced too soon after the shift change, the as yet unmanaged internal conflict caused by the shift change would have diverted the emotional and psychological energy required to cope with the trauma of the operating team change.

You must be prepared for interpersonal conflicts to spring up among your people. Do not overlook the reality that this is simply a reflection of the longing for contentment; do not allow its true meaning to be lost by deciding it is just another form of rebuff. Do not miss this opportunity for you to help others grow. The eventual successes of the shift change could not have accrued had I not been sensitive to the very real conflicts the idea produced among my people, and had I not tried to help each of them to put the whole issue in a perspective for each individual that he or she could perceive as being *right*.

As you assure conflict through change and provide coping mechanisms for that conflict, trust will grow. You will find others in the group have also begun to institute change and have also begun to help other people cope with conflict. This is the point when at least some of the people have begun to understand the tremendous potential of *conflict control*.

When this happens, you will be gratified by their willingness to share in the leadership process required for success, but you must remember that the process is never-ending and that it has not yet actually taken root with all of your people. You will still have to induce *many* of the needed changes yourself. It was for this reason that the bells continued to ring. They were still disliked, and the people were still focusing their frustrations on me, but the bells had subconsciously become a reminder for them to resist the longing for contentment as the means of achieving pride and dignity. At this point, we were at the end of month three of the experiment.

To establish a *conflict control* climate, you must: 1) decide to start, 2) accept and address negative reactions, and 3) use your instincts and reason to understand the behavior mechanism. A *conflict control* climate will cost little money to initiate, but it will cost much time, which you must be willing to invest. As people increasingly share in your leadership activities, you will need to devote less time. As you delegate more of your traditional duties, less traditional responsibility will burden you. You must prove you are trustworthy by visibly caring about people's needs and talents, and you must not prejudge or classify people by age, sex, ethnic group, personality, congeniality, previous judgments, or whatever.

The case study offers insight as to how I started and continued the *conflict control* experiment. You may find this insight helpful, but you must tailor your own approach to you and your company's situation. To accomplish this, you must sustain trust within yourself — trust in yourself and in other people. No one is likely to help you at first. Keep building on people's emerging strengths and keep focusing on their unearthed weaknesses. Always remember that human behavior is not an accurate indicator of the human potential that can actually be released.

As previously discussed, the classification of people demotivates them. Regarding the 5 percent of the people who are habitually nonproductive in a behavior control climate, you will find they probably will not be perceived as nonproductive in a *conflict control* climate that encourages them to grow — unless they think they are still being classified. In a *conflict control* climate, initially there probably *will* be 5 percent who are noticeably less productive and failing to heed the demands of the spirit. But the membership of this 5 percent will shift with changing circumstances. Nevertheless, vague patterns emerge as to how particular people will react under specific circumstances; these patterns can help you anticipate, and prepare to help minimize, the impact. Eventually you could end up with almost zero percent in normal circumstances. Classifying people invariably impairs the achievement of this potential, but it can always be rectified if it does not occur frequently.

In building trust, it is helpful to remember that trust can be betrayed unknowingly. Betrayal can be ascertained by informal discussions and then "reading between the lines." Eventually you will find a solution to each situation of this sort.

It is best not to expect immediate praise from the people you are attempting to help. People who are seeking contentment are quite uncomfortable with taking the risk of finding self-fulfillment. It is a threat to their "security." Praising you is the last thing they intend to do. Their comments will often reach you second- or third-hand. They will often seem childish and are not ego-building. These comments are unpleasant and may discourage you; but once you have deduced from them whatever you can, you must continue to forge ahead. You must not allow the the conflict such comments represent to lessen your resolve.

You also must expect that some of these comments will reach you through your boss. Spend a little extra time to ensure that more comments are not made by tracking some of them down to the source and confronting the perpetrator, but realize that you won't be totally successful.

Attempting to prevent inaccurate comments by being more formally or "scientifically" aware (a formal survey of your people's feelings and opinions, for example) will not disclose their real basis, especially since your people are not always the source (a surprising number of comments will originate outside your group). Trust your own instincts to yield clues for encouraging everybody to focus on achieving pride and dignity, rather than on counterproductive feelings. Your insights and perceptions will be even more helpful when attained through field observations and casual conversations. Unsolicited comments from outside the group occasionally may be helpful, but they usually tend to be disruptive.

Eventually, your boss will praise the quantitative performance of your people. This may be done with tongue in cheek if he or she is behavior control orientated. Finally, you will receive enthusiastic praise from your people. You will at that point — possibly a little before — become an inveterate convert, feeling confident that conflict control has taken firm root. At this point, we were at the end of month six in the experiment.

HOW TO PURSUE IT

Once trust has begun, remember that *conflict control* is a process that must be mentally reviewed periodically. It is a process of people helping one another to trust enough to give of their whole selves, thus achieving pride and dignity. It is integral to the synergism of people *striving for harmonious excellence*, which is the way of life that reflects the American heritage. Through this, people will achieve fulfillment (the pride and dignity of growth), thus optimizing productivity and quality. Governed by the behavior mechanism, it is a person's free will (when impacted by trust) that allows the demands of the spirit to optimize this process; it is the pursuit of one's destiny that justifies the process. Leadership is helping people to so behave and to thereby produce enrichment.

The case study offers some clues as to what is involved in the practice of *conflict control* and the underlying rationale segment offers some guidelines. Some of the precepts set forth in those two chapters may have been similar to those practiced elsewhere (although they may not actually have been articulated anywhere). You could locate, examine, and evaluate such practices in the context of the underlying rationale.

For example, Andrew Carnegie reportedly said, "The surest foundation of a business is quality; the effect of attention to quality upon every man cannot be overestimated, and that after quality — a long time after — comes cost." You might be able to determine how he pursued that precept, discovering some clues that might be applicable to your own situation.

Realistically, it may be simpler and more helpful to just follow your own intuition.

As you pursue *conflict control*, you will eventually encounter people's willingness to sacrifice personal needs in the interest of team needs. Such adult behavior extends even to situations where jobs will be eliminated. Even when people are bumped out of a group, the resulting trauma is minimized because those affected realize that it could not be avoided. They realize that they had helped make it happen, and that they would probably again become part of the group as soon as attrition or other circumstances allowed.

In the case study, the two people who left their jobs had been kept on longer than would have been expected. During that period they effectively helped in planning for further productivity gains, and they also helped others to realize the potential of the existing plans. Through being trusted to help others to trust, they left the plant with meaningful coping skills that would continue to serve them in any future conflicts. They were in a better position to pursue their destiny, thus playing a positive role in helping America to achieve its destiny.

Similar efforts to maintain trust need to be directed to former bosses who have become, instead, advisors with administrative responsibilities (i.e., the four function managers in the case study) as a consequence of *conflict control*. Even though their new roles may result in their often being consulted by past subordinates (as their innate *leadership* ability surfaces and evolves), they may continue to feel uncomfortable, and some may never completely resolve the uneasiness of no longer being part of their original group. A lot of trust is needed for them to believe in their growing worth, and to believe that *conflict control* does not basically change or threaten their career path. Thinking patterns and habits die hard, but they can be successfully subdued with enough trust.

Several people involved in the case study were promoted shortly after the end of the experiment. The technology manager became plant manager in another plant; the maintenance manager became the maintenance coordinator for a group of plants; and the quality manager became a quality specialist for a group of plants.

The production manager, however, went back to his former function as production foreman after I left the scene. Apparently this happened because the new plant manager, having decided to revert to the old type of plant management organization, either could not find a way to reward the production manager or did not have anyone else to fill the production foreman slot — or because the production manager simply *wanted* the production foreman slot.

Beyond the sorts of considerations that have just been discussed, the pursuit of *conflict control* fundamentally will rest with your allowing its practice to instinctively point to the direction of its next step.

In the case study, the plant unknowingly practiced portions of the many programs for productivity improvement that now exist. This seemed the natural thing to do; it was done by gut feel — without any edict or help from the top — and it was done without the knowledge that such programs existed (most of which didn't at that time). It was done without study of, or training in, the applicable precepts. Nevertheless, had such training been available, it would have been helpful; in pursuing *conflict control*, one should be alert to potentially helpful, existing training methods and management approaches.

Especially helpful would be formal training that would help a person to understand and accommodate others' values, styles, and needs, in spite of any personal differences or beliefs. Formal training in that arena is not ready to emerge anytime soon, because detailed knowledge of *all* of the intricacies of responding to the spirit apparently eludes comprehension — at least to the degree that detailed how-tos cannot be formulated (even though the general basics of the behavior mechanism, as articulated in the underlying rationale, seem obvious).

In spite of the many programs (such as participative management programs) dealing with limited facets of that challenge, it may be that only the instinctive approach to *conflict control* will be truly effective in helping us to grapple with understanding a person's behavior. It *may* be that any kind of training would not really help so much as education for all the people in the endeavor — education in history, literature, math, and science that would sharpen their instincts.

WHERE TO START IT

The pursuit of *conflict control* can begin anywhere. As previously suggested, its practice is inherently micro: two individuals, a team, or a group of teams (a *conflict control* unit); an entire organization would be a set of *conflict control* units, which individually are micro in scope (and would probably include cross-functional teams).

As discussed in the underlying rationale, the basic group for synergism is a team, and the basic unit for leadership assurance is the *conflict control* unit, made up of a single set of teams and their manager (in the case study, the plant was the *conflict control* unit). The number of people that should be involved is limited only by the manager's leadership ability — his or her ability to assure that the current needs of each of the individuals are met, and to assure any *conflict control* continuity that the teams may be unable to provide for themselves.

Obviously, support from the macro group, regardless of where in the organization the *conflict control* unit is located, would be helpful. One indirect form of such support would be the practice of *conflict control* by the other functions with which the *conflict control* unit interfaces (as in the good versus medium product situation illustrated in the case study), but this is not something that the unit alone can induce. The practice of *conflict control* at the top management level would similarly help, but its initial inception at that level of the organization might be untenable.

Nevertheless, because of *conflict control*'s impact on quantitative elements of profits, macro group support should entail more than just minimal sufferance. Perhaps the most useful form of such support, aside from widespread practice of *conflict control* in the macro group, is encouragement.

Beyond encouragement, in the obvious form of *recognition*, lies encouragement in a number of other forms. One form that would be quite helpful is tolerance of varied leadership styles. The critical need for such tolerance within the *conflict control* unit has already been suggested. For *conflict control* to start successfully, however, it would also be helpful if top management supported the personal leadership styles of the ones who start it. They will have to fall back on those styles (which may have been deeply submerged in the prior behavior control climate) frequently, albeit judiciously if they are to be credible in their efforts to build trust. Both the givers and receivers of such encouragement, however, need to be aware that any encouragement should be tendered as quietly as possible. When others in the hierarchy become aware of the situation, they will tend to view the switch to *conflict control* as threatening to their own control and security in the old behavior climate, which indeed it is. Their awareness should occur in a way and at a time that minimizes the perceived threat so that the success of the effort is not unnecessarily jeopardized.

Similar to tolerance, another form of useful encouragement is patience — patience for quantitative evidence of success. Trust takes time to build and a certain amount of chaos will be reflected in immature reactions, such as bickering within the group, which sometimes expands to complaints being heard outside the group. However, the quantitative evidence of success will seem to emerge quickly to anyone who has attempted to improve productivity through behavior control motivation. The time required to maintain such patience will vary, but it probably will range from between one month and one year. The case study example required three months.

The person who starts *conflict control* will also have to be patient for the same length of time before the *qualitative* evidence, derived from personal observations and one-on-one conversations, will disclose the beginnings of success.

Should the adoption of *conflict control* be decided at the top management level, but not implemented except at the lower management level, then a difficult situation presents itself and must be handled carefully (as previously noted). Since the decision probably was not adopted by the intervening levels, the initiating leaders will not be supported by the macro organization unless top management directly supports them.

It isn't that the intervening management levels may not want to support the initiators — particularly so in the interest of their status reports to top management — it is simply that, not strongly desiring to initiate it in their realm, they won't understand what is happening; therefore, they will not be able to cope with the confusion of the early stages of initiation. Their reports will be carefully worded, but probably will not be unconditionally supportive in terms of conclusions regarding the qualitative and quantitative performance of the group. Success is not necessarily foredoomed, but meaningful macro support *is* jeopardized unless the top boss is personally involved and is aware of the circumstances.

If the top boss anticipates this situation, he or she can set up a group of initiators from lower organization levels to work with him or her directly. The group can also be established after *conflict control* is otherwise initiated if the boss can identify the units that have made a good start. Assuming such a group is established, the boss and the initiators will need to communicate regularly. Perhaps this could be accomplished during a monthly half-day meeting, where information could be exchanged and suggestions could be made.

The hazards of this approach are obvious because the many levels of intervening people may feel threatened since their boss is bypassing them (which usually is verboten in a behavior control climate). The opportunities should also be obvious — the top boss will be seeing firsthand how *conflict control* can improve the bottom line at the real source of profits, will be learning how the process works, and will be discovering, or reinforcing, his or her own submerged compulsion to help people grow and to be helped to grow. The intent of this glimpse at the situation when starting *conflict control* at the top is not to suggest undue complexity, but rather to emphasize that *conflict control* cannot be edicted.

Although the opportunities of *conflict control do* involve risk, the only direct investments are time, desire, thought, and courage. Ultimately, the time required for leadership in a *conflict control* climate is less than the time required for managing people in a behavior control climate, and the former climate produces vastly superior results.

Although *conflict control* can start anywhere, it will reach the doers who produce the products (plant operators, field salesmen, etc.) more quickly if it begins at a lower organizational level. The lower on the ladder, however, the more layers there will be to cause its sudden demise, even long after it has taken root.

In the case study, *conflict control* began in a plant, which is fairly low in an industrial organization. It took root, and it survived. There was never any later attempt to kill it outright, because the bounties of the trust that unlocked the giving of whole selves were prodigious. Team trust was allowed to live, but without any further external nurturing. In another situation, however, its demise could have been edicted and enforced. This risk seems obvious, but it is nevertheless one that needs to be understood and accepted by those who would implement a *conflict control* climate.

Conflict control can begin anywhere. Encouragement helps it to survive. It is tricky to *start* it at the top management level and have it survive intact all the way through intervening layers to the bottom management level, but it is similarly complicated to *support* its survival from the top when it starts at the bottom.

BEYOND HOW AND WHERE

Beyond "how" and "where" are some implications that lie outside the constraints of this presentation. Some liberty with those constraints will now be taken by examining some of the other implications of *conflict control*.

The case study briefly mentioned two other plant developments — Job Scopes and EPAM. The basic framework of Job Scopes was noted, as was its reduction of a large organization to six layers. Should that sort of organizational structure be adopted, an entirely different kind of institution or segment of an institution (such as a corporation in industry) can be realistically envisioned as the next evolutionary step in pursuit of America's destiny. In such an organization, the top layer would be a distinctly separate group that would focus on corporate finance, technological expertise, societal relationships, business climate, etc. It would not be directly involved in the management of any of the *enrichment-producing* units (this excludes units that are basically administrative) of the endeavor.

Beyond the top layer, which can be called the core group, would lie a number of fundamentally independent businesses. The relationship between the core group and the businesses would be that the core group would consult, advise, and coordinate in matters such as communications, technology, finance, etc. This relationship would be sealed by a renewable contract, being negotiable every three to seven years. It would specify the what, how, and when of interchanges between the core group and the businesses; it would include the flow of capital from the core group to each business and the flow of profits from each business to the core group, probably shown as a percentage of the business' profits or losses. The businesses would otherwise be independent, each with its own personnel policies (possibly including EPAM), cost accounting systems, marketing strategies, raw material sources, etc.; but they would not be prohibited from cooperating with one another. In the realm of the routine operation of the endeavor, the core group would basically act as a financial institution.

This sort of approach would minimize the disruption of people's lives as the composition of the overall endeavor changed (as businesses joined and left the group). It could also separate money from motivation (to some degree) in routine decision making, thereby allowing each to be kept in better perspective regarding what and how Americans pursue their destinies. It would allow the *real* benefits of corporate bigness, yet would diminish its distortions. This would be enhanced if the core group somehow focused not only on the financial considerations, but also on education that would help people reduce the waste of human potential.

Noting the potential of this approach does not alter the enormous effort and risk taking that is required to arrive at such a goal, but it is clear that *conflict control* significantly eases the way by increasing the positive characteristics of creativity and dedication required for success, rather than intensifying the destructive, negative traits of skepticism and resistance.

Another implication of *conflict control* lies in the realm of the consumption of enrichment as opposed to the production of enrichment. Because *conflict control* produces behavior that reflects what individuals perceive to be *right*, it would minimize the overenrichment that greed secures; such overenrichment is no more *right* than any other behavior that does not comply to nature's plan. Should *conflict control* became deeply ingrained in the fabric of our society, this truth *would* become self-evident; people *would* find a way to *effectively* transfer their potential overenrichment to those who are underenriched.

We should also be aware that, since *conflict control* applies to all human beings, it may be embraced somewhere else before it is used in America. While it seems probable that our culture should be innately more amenable to the ultimate optimization of human relationships, the practice of *conflict control* is nevertheless *not* proprietarily American. In fact, Japan and other nations are already becoming more interested in creativity development and personal enrichment, and already seem to be taking some halting steps toward embracing the concept of *conflict control*.

Yet another implication of *conflict control* is philosophical in nature. That *conflict control* reflects American heritage has been stated many ways; what was not said, but may have seemed obvious, is that it reflects the particular religious bases on which American heritage evolved. For example, the "I am not my brother's keeper" nature of a behavior control climate is utterly alien to those bases. In contrast, *conflict control* presumes just the opposite. The practice of being our brother's keeper would prevent us from losing much of the true strength of our heritage; this may seem problematic, but the self-destructive implications of greed, in general, and behavior control, in particular, should *at least* be given serious thought.

In doing that, we need to ask ourselves why we originally became the masters of this continent — one that has so admirably allowed us to enrich ourselves and others? Similarly, why are we now trying to conquer the challenge of space? One aspect of the answer may be "because it is there." Another aspect of the answer — one that digs a little deeper — might be the "rightness" of it (in spite of some inevitable human mistakes in execution), or, conversely, "greed."

Which is the correct answer? If greed is correct, what are its implications of its finally becoming so entrenched that the longing for fulfillment is never reflected in human behavior — that pride and dignity are never achieved? And, if greed is not to be the case universally, where and in what institutions is it to be the case? Why is that so?

If rightness is the correct answer, is there anything about it that it could not continue to admirably guide us? What is the evidence that proves that it cannot?

One question leads to another, but the main purpose of our focusing on the religious nature of American heritage is simply to parallel its implications with those of *conflict control*. Each person must draw his or her own conclusion regarding the validity and relevancy of the argument. The depth of our dilemma suggests that we should seriously consider the proposition that "thoughtful consideration of human aspirations" is absolutely essential to being human, in contrast to "mindless support of misunderstandings" of what that may really mean.

SUMMARY

The full utilization of the strengths of people stems from satisfying their longing for fulfillment. This can be done only through *striving for harmonious excellence* through the process of *conflict control*. This process can be initiated by anyone who desires to do so, but it must begin with the building of trust.

Beyond that, its successful initiation depends on people focusing on accommodating each other's perceptions of *right*. The reality that such accommodations are essential to the optimization of the creation of wealth and profits through people has eluded us so far. Nevertheless, it can be embraced through leadership.

Once *conflict control* is initiated, its pursuit is basically instinctive, with the process itself pointing the way. As it is pursued, the required leadership is increasingly assumed by each of the practitioners. At this point, its success depends only on its being allowed to survive. In spite of its astounding results, its survival cannot be guaranteed in an environment where the macro organization is typified by a behavior control climate. Great care must be exercised in external corporate or departmental relations. External support can be helpful, but it is not essential.

The spread of *conflict control* into the fabric of American society would assure not only the optimization of the creation of wealth (and profits) in today's business endeavors, but it would also help us to reshape the framework of our institutions in such a way that the future creation of wealth would be enhanced, and the achievement of our individual and collective destinies would be assured.

CHAPTER 5

HOW THE PROCESS WORKS

GENERAL

The key thoughts following are a preparation for the discussion of how the process works. Some have been previously mentioned and all are more fully developed in the underlying rationale.

We will examine: 1) the relationship of a doer and a helper, 2) the basic role of goals as proscribed by that relationship, 3) the usefulness of properly developed team goals to optimize the creation of the wealth, and 4) an example of how the process works. We must realize that for goals to be useful, there must be a trust level that can be accrued only through the give and take of *conflict control* (which includes leadership that does not allow one's style, values, or circumstances to get in the way of success).

To optimize the creation of wealth, the giving of one's whole self is essential. All such acts of giving are inherently equal even though *what* is given and *how* it is given will vary in different situations and between individuals. All individuals need help from time to time to build the trust required to give of themselves.

PROBLEMS

In practicing these precepts, there is a commonly held misconception that makes the effort more difficult. It reflects confusion as to the nature of productive competition. The flaw is the notion that winning an objective is all that matters and that how it is pursued is immaterial.

This misconception embraces various slogans, such as survival of the fittest; I am not my brother's keeper; and winning is everything. It follows from our precepts that such slogans or viewpoints are incorrect justifications of behavior for one who would optimize the creation of wealth. Such slogans ignore our basic behavior mechanism which requires us to help others to be productive and fulfilled.

The case study suggested that even at the team level, one team cannot justify its behavior at the expense of another team's growth. It is not that individuals or teams do not excel at some activity more than others, because they do; similarly, others will excel at some other activity. We must remember that excellence is a fluctuating, dynamic condition. What is important is that those who strive to excel are not merely trying to "outperform" others, but, rather, that they are trying to achieve *harmonious excellence* through real competition, thus achieving personal growth and/or producing enrichment for everyone involved.

As defined, excellence truly enriches people. In an athletic event, for example, growth is the pride and dignity of developing and using one's physical, mental, and emotional skills in performing an exercise. Enrichment could be the satisfaction of the spectators' growth needs. Excellence is the competitive expertise (professionalism) with which the exercise is performed.

Harmonious excellence is comprised of three elements: 1) the chosen objectives — i.e., outmaneuvering a defensive guard may help a running back effectively use his skills or help his team score more points than the other football team, and 2) how the objectives are achieved — which plays are called and how they are executed. It excludes doing whatever is perceived as not *right*. Circumventing the blocker in a football game by faking him out will probably be perceived as *right*; deliberately injuring his leg to reduce his effectiveness will be perceived as not *right*.

Deliberately injuring a player's leg also breaks a football rule and, if caught, the perpetrator's team will be penalized. That point is not relevant to the argument except as a reminder that rules are simply a form of behavior control which, among other things, ensconces people in boxes (behind which they can hide) to exploit their longing for contentment, as previously discussed. It encourages them to conform to a status quo rather than to grow. Rules foreclose on people's longing for fulfillment, on their behavior as accountable adults, and on their achievement of pride and dignity — whether in the interest of corporate profits or athletic victories. "Don't get caught" is the inevitable and degrading advice given by those who are enslaved by rules and tend to look the other way.

There is nothing inherently wrong with profits and winning, but when the "how" is ignored as a condition, then profits and winning are counterproductive as justification for the activities of human beings. They are also utterly un-American. Some may consider the previously noted slogans or mores as being "American as apple pie," but they are, in fact, diametrically opposed to the very basis of our heritage. The reason this is not always clearly perceived may reflect confusion about the meaning of America being a nation of laws and not of men. The popular interpretation that we have license to do whatever is not illegal is incorrect. It is precisely in the realm of what is not covered by common consent laws (rules of behavior) that we, as human beings, are supposed to seek our destinies. As the underlying rationale pointed out, this involves helping each other, not exploiting each other.

Classification is another problem when applying these precepts to the doer-helper relationship. It seems to be integral to the counterproductive form of competition. Although it has been discussed previously, I will briefly highlight its danger in the arena of competitive team interaction.

First, however, let us note that individuals or teams may strive for the same excellence simultaneously when pursuing an objective (for example, zero defects in the case study). This can lead to judgment by management as to their comparative expertise. Judgment is probably inevitable, and when it is not followed by classification it can help those with less expertise or success to improve, and/or it can help those with more expertise or success to help others.

Differences will always exist in what is contributed and how it is contributed. However, this may cloud the perception of the true growth or excellence achieved. It also clouds the insight as to true relative success. Excellence is relative only to something external (an athletic record or a competitor's performance, etc.), but the growth of a participant is relative only to his or her achieved degree of pride and dignity, and is the direct product of striving to do something that is *right* in a way that is *right*.

The only crucial determinant of optimizing the creation of wealth will be that everyone harmoniously strived to achieve excellence; the only justification of the endeavor will be that such striving occurred.

If the team that focused on housekeeping in the case study had not also striven for quality before the other teams met its housekeeping standard, than zero quality defects would never have been achieved. Similarly, if the team that focused on quality had not striven for housekeeping, then the plant's housekeeping performance would have been poorer. But if both teams had striven in all facets of plant operation, then zero defects as well as housekeeping excellence would both have been achieved. *Striving for harmonious excellence* would have optimized the creation of wealth. Thus, the striving *attempt* is the key that unlocks the door to *harmonious excellence*.

Nevertheless, the quality team's housekeeping efforts may still have been judged to be less successful than the housekeeping team's housekeeping efforts, while its quality efforts may have been judged to be more successful. It is not always (perhaps not ever) possible to avoid making such judgments, but judgments can lead to counterproductive behavior nonetheless. For example, if the judgments were made in a behavior control climate, the boss would next try to impose the performance of the most successful team — the "winners" — on the others — the "losers" — of the competition. He or she would first classify the "losers" as careless, however, to get their attention and to help himself or herself focus the additional behavior control that he or she would certainly impose. This will be done even if the losers had performed better than ever before, and it will guarantee that future performance of both teams will deteriorate, of course.

Understanding the true nature of competition can help us avoid the error of classification. Should the error nevertheless be committed in a *conflict control* climate, it will not cause performance to regress *completely* if sufficient trust exists, but it *will diminish* the level of trust and the creation of wealth, and thus performance. On the other hand, if the judgment is not allowed to become a classification, it can be useful as a guideline for what kind of help should be provided.

Help can take the form of public or private recognition. In the case study, the team that focused on safety won praise in the local company newsletter. The team that focused on output earned a letter of recognition at the corporate level and thus earned company-wide respect, including the safety team's gratitude for the respect it gained by association. The safety team's gratitude was genuine, but they no doubt must have wondered whether a corporate letter or recognition was also going to be written for safety performance. Recognition is important, but it is complex and must be exercised carefully to be truly helpful.

In summary, *optimizing the creation of wealth* results from *striving for harmonious excellence* and making *conflict control* a way of business life. Classification is voided and "anything-goes" competition is recognized as counterproductive, but true competition is recognized as a growth agent. The enterprise that then emerges (entrepreneurship, creativity, acceptance of the risk of change) is the true hallmark of free enterprise — of freedom from behavior control and its constraint on trust.

Once trust is established, the *doer-helper relationship* allows each person to communicate empathetically with the other person, understanding the other's position as much as possible. As noted in the underlying rationale, the other person's terms revolve around the basic satisfaction of his or her needs. The clear perception of those needs puts one in the other's place, which is permitted only through mutual trust. This helps the other person to strive for the satisfaction of only those needs that he or she perceives as *right* in terms of the objectives pursued and the methods used. It is applicable to both the doer and the helper, and it does not matter who is the one and who is the other.

EXAMPLE

The doer-helper relationship typically begins with the helper observing the doer's behavior and deducing that certain aspects of that behavior may be a reflection of the doer's insecurity intensifying. It could be a look on the doer's face, mistakes in job execution, or some other manifestation of discord; or it could begin with the doer asking for help.

The first thing the helper does in the doer-helper relationship is to observe evidence of discord; then the helper probably makes a judgment regarding the nature of the evidence. It may be, for example, that the doer is not keeping his or her work area neat even though he or she appears to have time to do so. Being careful not to mentally classify the doer as being sloppy, careless, or having a poor attitude, and realizing that the observed clutter does not represent in itself a significant danger requiring immediate action, the observer should wait before taking action. The observer should take some time to consider what the root cause of the clutter might be, and what action might be taken in order to help. This is the point where the observer has become a helper.

Later, the same sort of clutter may be observed again. Let's assume a small pool of oil was on the floor near the doer's machine and was caused by a leak in the machine's oil reservoir tank outlet. The helper noticed, however, that the machine was running beautifully; this brought to mind the doer's proud reputation as a fine machine operator.

The helper decided to take action. The helper could have mentioned the situation to someone else or cleaned up the oil, but the helper decided to mention the oil pool to the doer. He or she could have used various approaches in confronting the doer; he or she might or might not give them some advance thought.

For example, the helper probably would not have considered the implications of saying, "You're sloppy, clean up that oil." If the helper were to say that, one thing would have led to another, and the next day another pool of oil would have resulted from that classifying admonishment. If the helper had persisted in that vein long enough, but really was trying to help, he or she would first need to receive some help in interpersonal communications. If the helper had persisted, but was not really trying to help, he or she may have been the boss in a behavior control climate.

If the helper were the boss, he or she probably would then have issued an edict that oil pools must be cleaned up immediately, accompanied by instructions as to how to do it and a schedule for oil cleanup. For as long as the boss cared to check for oil pools, he or she could be assured that oil pools were being cleaned up. He or she probably would have to also edict how the material used to clean up the oil will be disposed of, by whom, and when. That would be followed by another edict regarding the conservation of the material used for cleaning up oil. The boss would conclude again that people do not care about doing a good job, and their behavior will indeed support that conclusion; this self-fulfilling prophecy will tend to breed failure ad infinitum. He or she would be unaware of the ensuing decline in productivity and quality until the end-of-month cost sheets were reviewed. Even at that time, the boss would still be unaware of the qualitative parameters that had governed productivity and quality, but he or she *would* be alarmed at the decline in the quantitative measures of performance. The boss may relate this productivity information solely to the cost of oil cleanup as he or she prepared explanations for his or her superior. Hopefully, he or she would be able to present them during a housekeeping inspection tour with his or her boss!

The damaged qualitative parameters of productivity and quality (creativity, dedication, pride, and dignity) would continue to be reflected in performance, but the boss would only be able to perceive the deteriorated performance as somehow being another cost of cleaning up oil. Distortion of reality would tend to breed greater distortion of reality.

The helper may or may not have considered the implications of asking, "When do you plan to clean up that oil?" Let's assume that that is what the helper said. At this point we will assume the doer will acquiesce to the helper's need to help by allowing the conversation to meaningfully continue by saying, "What oil?" The helper had similarly acquiesced to the doer by selecting an approach that allowed the doer to meaningfully respond; both have taken a step that was, in effect, *striving for harmonious excellence through conflict control* through trust.

The helper may then say, "That oil!" The doer may reply, "Oh, that; that's nothing; I didn't even know it was there. What's your problem?" The helper may briefly feel like snapping, "You know our standards around here. Were you born in a pig sty?" But wanting to help, the helper would consciously or subconsciously reject that as an incorrectly perceived need.

The helper instead may respond, "I don't have any problem, but it looks to me like that oil is hazardous." The doer may respond with, "I haven't slipped yet and neither has anyone else." The helper may say, "Yeah, but sooner or later someone will. Besides, that oil isn't up to our housekeeping standards."

At that point, the practice of *conflict control* has failed. The ensuing argument about subjective standards and obligations will never be resolved, and the interpersonal conflict will remain temporarily unresolved.

Assuming sufficient trust survived, the pass of time will allow another opportunity for discussion. Perhaps a coffee break occurs at that moment and the walk to the coffee machine provides the needed time. The helper may say, "It looks like there's no way we're going to agree on what our housekeeping standard really is — particularly since we eliminated all the old written standards last year. But I did hear a couple of people mention the oil this morning, and I got the feeling that they thought you should clean it up." The doer's response may be, "Who were they?" The helper may say, "It doesn't really matter; they were really talking about how our team could do a better job of housekeeping and — oh, by the way, they really were impressed with your production record last week." The helper may then hear, "Yeah, well it's easy for them to talk about cleaning up oil — they don't have to do it!" After a pause, the doer may say, "Tell you what — let me give it some thought."

In providing the doer with the objective of improving his or her team's housekeeping, the helper's striving finally came up with an objective the doer could perceive as right. The next day, however, the helper observed another pool of oil. The doer may say, "Whoops, I started to clean that up twice already, but then got busy with something else. I've got to figure out a way to remember to clean it up — how about watching my machine for a second while I go get some rags?" When the doer returns, the helper may say, "I know what you mean — I've got the same problem remembering to check the oil level on my machine." Then, "Yeah, I heard your low oil level alarm go off yesterday, but I was right in the middle of changing my oil filters and couldn't get over right away to help you. You know, maybe we need to figure out some sort of a schedule to do these things."

One of them may develop a schedule that works for him or her, and the other may also try it. At some point, each person, with or without help from others — will have found a way that works and seems *right*. The problem will have been solved, the two parties will have increased their trust in each other, each will have achieved pride and dignity, and each will have become more productive (one less slipping hazard and one more adequately lubricated machine). The quality of life will have improved on the job. Product quality also will improve as the result of fewer operating disruptions (fewer falls and less frequent machine downtime).

The quality of life and operational productivity and quality will have increased because of the trust that resulted from the doer and helper relating to each other's terms, values, and styles in the practice of *conflict control*. They both strived for *harmonious excellence*; their next encounter will be settled more expeditiously because their additional trust will reduce the amount of preliminary verbal sparring.

COMMENTS

Each previous step of the process could have taken countless other paths. There is no way to predict the specific goals or objectives that would have been selected, the particular methods that would have been chosen, or the output that would have been achieved — but, productivity, quality, and fulfillment *would* have been enhanced to *some* degree.

In the example cited, someone other than the helper or the doer might have later arranged for the leak to be fixed. From a cost accounting or mechanical engineering viewpoint, that might have been more desirable. From the doer's and helper's point of view, however, this might not have been as personally satisfying since they had together found pride and dignity through interpersonal communication. If they had not been involved in the considerations that led to the decision to repair the leak, their level of trust for all people might have been diminished. Had their achievement been genuinely recognized by management — especially if they had been involved in the "repair" decision — their level of trust would have been enhanced and would have enhanced the future creation of wealth.

When and where such future dividends will accrue cannot be predicted; some might even be realized outside the place of work in the community (another institution's gain, however, is not necessarily the workplace institution's loss). For example, one of the individuals may have felt good enough about himself or herself for what he or she had achieved at work, that he or she took on additional community volunteer work in the community, or he or she might have taken a friend out to dinner, or whatever.

The only clue about the exact dividend that can be expected would be the relative size (of the dividend) that can be expected. That clue occupies a position in a spectrum. The clue could be comments. For example, it could be the doer's and helper's future comments regarding oil leaks. They range from, "Let's run an even cleaner shop" at one end of the spectrum, through no comments at all, to, "I can't help you because I've got to clean up an oil leak" at the other end. Tenuous as they may seem, in reality clues of that sort are vital to a business' success and creation of wealth through its people, for they are the only meaningful indicators of one of the countless simple and mundane achievements that together comprise enormous success and wealth.

Beyond such situations lie the major changes of the sort illustrated by the shift change in the case study. It may well be that both sort of changes (mundane and traumatic) are required for optimization of the creation of wealth in many endeavors.

EXPECTATIONS

One thing is certain. There will be future oil leaks that do not get cleaned up immediately. *Conflict control* does not assure perfection — immediate or otherwise. It simply is a process that is essential to growth. Growth is accompanied by behavior that enhances performance and that allows expectations to realistically rise.

As long as *conflict control* is practiced, the whole cycle will continue to spiral upward; but each time a pool of oil is promptly cleaned up, people will need to cope with the attendant conflict that arises. This can be facilitated if people distinguish between goals and realistic expectations.

Goals should represent the upgrading of the present condition, but not necessarily represent a state of perfection. Expectations should focus on the rate of progress toward the goal. In the example, zero oil leaks can be visualized, as can zero elapsed time between leak and cleanup. Visualizing such perfection is extremely important, but care must be exercised in translating the vision into a goal. For example, which of the two noted visualizations should become the goal? Is one drop of oil in 10 years to be considered a leak? If so, how will it be detected? When? By whom? Are two drops of oil a pool? Or are 20 drops of oil? How big is a drop? If 20, is the cleanup prompt when the twentieth drop falls to the floor — or just before the twenty-first drop falls?

Visualization serves a legitimate purpose. Goals can help the ultimate realization of the vision, but expectations are the essential basis of success. However, *ambiguity* of expectations invites failure. The imperfect nature of measurements (how big is a drop, and how is it to be measured?) consequently should assure that great care be taken when formulating expectations, especially if they are to be written down in spite of the dynamic nature of the real world.

Similarly, goals should never be considered as having been cast in bronze just because they are written, and visualizations of what might be perhaps should never be written down. The problem with writing goals is that they are usually used by the manager as a standard of measurement of the person's performance regardless of who writes them or with what intent. The problem is that goals deal with the future, but the interim is unpredictable. The usual approach is to set a quantified goal. Since the interim circumstances are unpredictable, the goal will either not be met, or will be so certain of success that it will not represent an achievement of anything near the potential achievement. Thus, the person who is saddled with the goal is doomed to either fail or to strive for something trivial.

However, each person should write his or her own *private* work goals to help assure that some such goals exist. Each person will know how he or she is doing in terms of achieving goals, and peers and the manager will sense if he or she is giving of his or her whole self. This applies to teams as well as to individuals.

In a *conflict control* climate, everyone has visions for betterment (visions are products of giving of one's whole self); most of the more productive goals are not written down, and expectations are kept realistic through the give and take inherent in the doer-helper relationship. The imprecision of evidence of the creation of wealth is intuitively understood.

Briefly, my point in discussing written goals is that we must remember that they are tricky to administer, they can be ambiguous regarding realistic expectations, they can be misleading if they are a measure of people's performance, and they may be unnecessary in a *conflict control* climate.

Nevertheless, there is nothing *inherently* wrong with quantitatively, precisely, and *productively* measuring something that can be measured. In the case study, the zero defects discussed were zero by the traditional method of measurement, but may not have been zero by more rigorous, available methods of measurement. The quality (specification conformance) variability of the products shipped, however, always *seemed* to satisfy the customers' needs. Therefore a more rigorous method of measurement was not used since the time required to achieve a more rigorous goal might have been better spent pursuing other worthwhile objectives for increasing wealth and profit.

Nevertheless, customer satisfaction is both subtle and dynamic. Not accumulating a more *precise*, measurements-based history of production variation and shipment quality may have unnecessarily risked our not meeting the customer's current true expectations and future needs. We may never know if that risk was, in fact, unnecessary.

In general, precise measures of quantifiable variability are indispensable strategies for effectively achieving progress. In the oil pool example, one might begin by plotting the frequency with which large pools of oil were not promptly cleaned up. If everyone involved agreed the measurements were practical and informative, if a control chart was used to plot the data, and if the technical precepts of SQC were rigorously practiced, then the frequency of pools of oil eventually could be reduced. This could be accomplished by setting up a maintenance schedule, by investigating a particular step in the machine's operation, or by utilizing *whatever* indications the technical information uncovers. This could result in less frequent oil leaks and/or smaller pool sizes. This would occur optimally (in terms of time) in a *conflict control* climate *within* the dynamic priorities of the overall endeavor and those of the concerned individuals or teams.

Even without an approach such as SQC, a *conflict control* climate would tend to succeed in reducing variability (this is how zero defects was achieved in the case study). This is true because variability reduction and excellence both fight all waste within a business or factory, including the waste of human resources. *Conflict control*'s leadership, of course, focuses first on waste of human resources through people *striving for harmonious excellence*. In focusing on excellence, that leadership necessarily focuses on realistic, priority-driven expectations for the progress that is required for true excellence. People in a *conflict control* climate *instinctively* know when action needs to be taken to optimize the creation of wealth because they work for the common good, not for ego satisfaction. They "know" what *all* of the needs of the organization are.

In contrast, variability in a behavior control climate will not be tackled as effectively because the boss will edict absolutes and will attempt to achieve them through the imposition of behavior controls, as noted in the oil pool example. Simply and naturally reducing variability is completely foreign to the boss' approach; but should he or she perceive that SQC can reduce costs, the boss will force it on his or her people and will use behavior control to try to ensure that the sources of variability are eliminated. Consequently, the boss will ignore the resultant waste of human potential (which, being qualitative, cannot be plotted quantitatively), thereby ultimately assuring he or she will have to absolutely control improvement design and implementation. This will be true not only in the 85 percent variability that is usual for the overall system, but also in the 15 percent range where, for example, the boss will try to make plant operators reduce their product variability.

In isolated situations, SQC could initially achieve statistical progress faster through behavior control's dictated absolutes than it could through *conflict control*'s priorities, but through its use of human potential the *conflict control* climate would quickly close the gap and take the lead.

Nothing in the technical aspects of SQC, typified by control charts, will inherently cause a boss to abandon behavior control. Also, nothing inherently exists in the broader aspects of SQC, typified by the "stop using fear" dictum, that will inherently cause a boss or the macro organization to abandon profit-driven behavior control.

Both the narrow (statistics) and broad (people) aspects of SQC foretell prosperity. *How* the broad aspects accomplish it and how people amplify the narrow aspects are not obvious and must be believed. In a behavior control climate, people as resources can always be manipulated to show reduced cost on monthly cost sheets, therefore dooming SQC's broad potential to abandonment, and its narrow potential to diminution by nonbelievers.

OBSERVATIONS

Even though the practice of *conflict control* seems to take a lot of time, one should always keep in mind its potential. The example, for instance, may give the impression that the doer-helper relationship required too much time, and certainly it took more time than if the situation had been simply ignored. However, a total of only two or three man-hours were needed to reach the point where oil cleanup and lubrication schedules were actually established and future success had been enhanced. The behavior control boss, on the other hand, would have needed at least the same amount of time to write, publish, and distribute his or her initial edicts; and, instead of finding success, he or she would have ensured failure.

Had the situation been more complex by directly involving more people, more time would have been required in both approaches; there would have been more opportunity to assure either more future success or more future failure. In the most complex situations, it is conceivable that the traditional approach of behavior control would not allow the boss enough time to even devise a solution to the problem much less to actually solve it. In using traditional methods to save our preeminence as a nation in an increasingly complex world, America may be fast approaching that sort of dilemma.

It may also have seemed that the helper was simply lucky, merely stumbling upon a successful approach. The case study practitioners, however, found that as practicing *conflict control* became more natural, their apparent stumbling increasingly was successful, which suggests that success breeds success and that luck is not a major component.

The conversations in the example may have seemed familiar (they certainly were simple and natural); similar discussions can be found in all workplaces. Their universal occurrence verifies them as a natural form of human relationship, but their productivity is masked and their occurrence is limited in a behavior control climate.

The *conflict control climate is* simple and natural (but not necessarily easy) to achieve, as are the skills required to implement it. No special abilities are required (but meaningful training and education for those who could benefit would definitely make it *easier* to achieve).

Even so, *conflict control* is not characteristic of most climates. It isn't that most people don't have a need to help — because everyone does. It is that a behavior control climate emphasizes people performance predictability and, hence, quantified job expectations, thus playing to our passion for measuring. It squelches visible difficulties, interpersonal conflict, and nonconformance with its so-called culture, thereby suppressing the give and take of the doer-helper relationship, and diminishing the potential of *any* external help that may be rendered.

In addition to suppressing individual creativity and accountability, the destructive restraints of a behavior control climate also hamper multi-institutional efforts — i.e., research joint ventures by industry, academia, and government. The group members in such a situation will perform only the roles assigned by their institution (like the product management team in the case study), will avoid interpersonal conflict and personal accountability, and will fail to achieve creativity. Each individual representative of his or her institution will have no option other than to look inward for justification, and this leads to insecurity and greed.

This is so because — others having denied them trust — the longing for contentment (for the status quo, for freedom from conflict, for freedom from accountability) overwhelms them. They inevitably focus on greed for satisfying their need for justification — believing that money or power can justify denying the demands of the spirit and may satisfy their longing for contentment. It never does, for it is the evolving needs of nature that always prevail.

Therefore, it is not surprising, but nonetheless tragic, that those who achieve the most money or power through greed are so often "honored" by people who aspire to emulate them or who see in them the justification of their own attempts (tragically denying themselves the real justification of pride and dignity, of fulfillment, of growth). As a result of this sort of alienation from our heritage, we Americans are losing our preeminence as a nation, and will never regain it as long as this sort of selfishness persists — as long as we allow greed or fear to cause us to subjugate others or to be subjugated by others.

SUMMARY

The process of *conflict control* works by allowing and, when necessary, helping natural human relationships to flourish and to develop on their own. The key to accomplishing this is trust. The major threat is behavior control (which is a product of misconceptions about human relationships and conflict). Absolute conformance to misguided behavior control regulations and systems is the basic antithesis of the realistic expectations and accommodating characteristics of the *conflict control* process.

TRAITS AND REQUIREMENTS

We need to reexamine the way we go about deciding the why, what, when, and how of living; we can accomplish this only by focusing on opportunities to become more realistic in our human relationships. The only needed traits to do this are our desire to do so, the decency and wisdom to do what we know is *right*, and the courage to see it through. These traits can be found within us all.

The only needed requirements for using those traits will be for each of us to simply go ahead and use them wherever and whenever possible (without waiting to be told), and for us to be allowed to do so (which is possible if we are careful and determined). The former is something each of us can do, and the latter is something we all can assume.

Will we make such an effort? The answer, of course, is within each of us; there are no compelling or fundamental reasons why any one of us should not.

If we do, when will we? That answer, too, is to be found within each of us; it would be better to reverse our current trend sooner rather than later, of course, but certainly before it is *too* late.

Why do it? That answer is one that each of us knows with absolute certainty — regardless of how deep it is buried in us and how painful the search for it might be. I believe that for each of us the answer immutably is "because I must."

INDEX

Behavior control:
  definition of, 1
  nature of, xii, 11, 34-39

Boss: nature of, 34-36, 42-43

Classification of people:
  definition of, 2
  nature of, 18, 33-34, 60-61

Competition: productive versus nonproductive, 59-62

Conflict control:
  beginning of, 46
  concepts of, 13
  definition of, 3
  nature of, xii, 8, 11, 18, 35-36, 43-45, 54, 57, 69-70

Conflict control unit:
  definition of, 52
  nature of, 52

Contentment: nature of, 6-7

Destiny:
  America: alienation from, x, 69-70
    hope for, xiv
    nature of, 13
  definition of, 2
  individual: hope for, xiv
    nature of, 13, 32, 45

Dignity:
  definition of, 3
  source of, x, 6, 10

Excellence (*see* Harmonious excellence)

Free will:
  definition of, 2
  nature of, 5